The School Counselor's Guide to ADHD

To my loving wife, Linda, and my grandchildren, Brianna and Nicholas, who have brought a special joy to my life.

—Richard A. Lougy

This book is dedicated to the loving memory of Deborah A. Ackerman. Her love for life, encouragement, and constant intercession gave me the courage and strength to continue in the endeavor to be a "voice for the voiceless." Her support and encouragement have been a true gift to my life.

—Silvia L. DeRuvo

To Marci and Alex, with love.

—David Rosenthal

The School Counselor's Guide to ADHD

What to Know and Do to Help Your Students

Richard A. Lougy
Silvia L. DeRuvo
David Rosenthal, MD

CORWIN
A SAGE Company

KH

For information:

Corwin
A SAGE Company
2455 Teller Road
Thousand Oaks, California 91320
(800) 233-9936
Fax: (800) 417-2466
www.corwinpress.com

SAGE Ltd.
1 Oliver's Yard
55 City Road
London EC1Y 1SP
United Kingdom

SAGE Pvt. Ltd.
B 1/I 1 Mohan Cooperative
   Industrial Area
Mathura Road, New Delhi 110 044
India

SAGE Asia-Pacific Pte. Ltd.
33 Pekin Street #02-01
Far East Square
Singapore 048763

Printed in the United States of America

Library of Congress Cataloging-in-Publication Data

Lougy, Richard A., 1944-
The school counselor's guide to ADHD: what to know and do to help your students / Richard A. Lougy, Silvia L. DeRuvo, David Rosenthal.
    p. cm.
Includes bibliographical references and index.
ISBN 978-1-4129-6652-8 (cloth)
ISBN 978-1-4129-6653-5 (pbk.)

   1. Attention-deficit-disordered children—Education—United States. 2. Attention-deficit-disordered children—Counseling of—United States. 3. Attention-deficit-disordered children—Drug use—United States. 4. Hyperactive children—Counseling of—United States. 5. Educational counseling—United States 6. Attention-deficit hyperactivity disorder—United States. I. DeRuvo, Silvia L. II. Rosenthal, David. III. Title.

LC4713.4.L68 2009
371.94—dc22   2009007519

This book is printed on acid-free paper.

09   10   11   12   13   10   9   8   7   6   5   4   3   2   1

Acquisitions Editor:	Jessica Allan
Editorial Assistant:	Joanna Coelho
Production Editor:	Veronica Stapleton
Copy Editor:	Codi Bowman
Typesetter:	C&M Digitals (P) Ltd.
Proofreader:	Dennis W. Webb
Indexer:	Molly Hall
Cover Designer:	Rose Storey
Graphic Designer:	Scott Van Atta

6/27/11

Contents

Preface

*T*he *School Counselor's Guide to ADHD* will help school counselors find ways to work more effectively with children with attention-deficit/hyperactivity disorder (ADHD) in the school environment.

It is intended to serve as a practical how-to guide for counselors with little or no experience working with children with ADHD and also for more knowledgeable counselors who need to refresh their knowledge or are interested in learning more about this disorder. Other readers who encounter children with ADHD on a regular basis, including school psychologists and school administrators, will find this book helpful. The information in this book can also be of value to students and trainees working on their administrative, school psychology, and school counseling credentials.

School counselors will find this book useful because it outlines challenges they may encounter while working with these special students. It is geared toward school-based treatment in contrast to agency-based treatment programs for children with ADHD. Schools are often skipped over by outside professionals when treating these special children. However, schools may be the only setting where treatment is available for many families of children with ADHD because of financial considerations or, for some, personal resistance to outside psychotherapy because of the stigma still associated with seeing a mental health specialist. Families who have the financial resources to access private psychotherapy services are often, but not always, better acquainted with support services in the community and better educated than those who seek help at public treatment programs. Consequently, many families with limited resources look primarily to the child's doctor or the school to help their child be more successful.

We will be describing an integrated multimodal approach to working with children with ADHD that is pragmatic, nondogmatic, and user friendly. Among the hallmarks of our approach are (a) the importance of communicating with other caregivers and professionals who work with the child; (b) maintaining a spirit of collaboration with the teacher, parents, and children; and (c) maintaining a positive, optimistic stance that instills hope and empowers the teacher, parents, and child even when they experience setbacks, disappointments, and mistakes.

The population of children with ADHD is heterogeneous, and contrary to popular stereotypes, children with ADHD differ from one another in many ways. Academic and behavioral interventions need to be tailored to the child's individual needs. Accordingly, children with ADHD must be approached in different ways, and it is impossible to know in advance what will be the best approach in working with each child. As an educator, you must have an open mind, a flexible attitude, a willingness to go with the flow or change directions when needed, and, frankly, be adventurous and realize that interventions are often guided by trial and error. The key is to figure out what works best for a particular child at a particular point in time. To be successful, school counselors and support staff need a menu of different options to choose from. There is no one best treatment method or approach for everyone with ADHD.

The only guideline we encourage is that educators do what appears to work best for the particular child they are seeing. If you are looking for a cookbook method, this book is not for you. What we offer are helpful suggestions, guidelines, and techniques that you can use as you work with these special children. But these techniques will need to be adapted and modified to fit the child with whom you are working. We hope that what you read in this book will empower you to more freely exercise your own judgment and release your thinking from the confines of past approaches, many of which claimed to be the one and only effective way to deal with children with ADHD.

Acknowledgments

We first want to thank all the teachers and other school staff (e.g., administrators, school secretaries, custodians, cafeteria staff, and other helpful school personnel) who often are not generally recognized for the hard work and dedication to the jobs that they perform. We also would be remiss in not thanking those children and families who have taught us so much about best practices in working with children with ADHD. Parents have opened their hearts to us in hopes of helping their children. Acknowledging that a child needs the help of a professional is not easy to accept by any parent, and we recognize and appreciate this trust. The responsibility parents shoulder in battling for the needs of their children with ADHD is not taken lightly, and we appreciate their confidence in us.

Our knowledge and understanding of this disorder rests on the backs of those professionals who have brought, through research and dedication, important understanding of ADHD and how it can negatively impact a child's social and educational development.

Last, we want to thank those advocates, organizations, and other professionals that have brought this disorder to the attention of educators. Many have had to fight courageously and mercilessly in hopes of dispelling erroneous notions held by many in education about ADHD. One important avenue was provided by Corwin. Without their belief in our mission, we may not have had the opportunity to share our expertise. Through their guidance and support, this book has come to fruition.

We cannot fail to acknowledge the editorial staff at Corwin, two of whom provided special guidance and support, Jessica Allan and Codi Bowman. Their professional insight and support made this adventure a gratifying endeavor.

Corwin wishes to acknowledge the following peer reviewers for their editorial insight and guidance.

Dr. Joseph C. Ciechalski
Counselor Educator
East Carolina University
Greenville, NC

Gloria Avolio DePaul, PhD
Nationally Board Certified School Counselor
Hillsborough County School District
Tampa, FL

Kylie P. Dotson-Blake, PhD, LPC, NC School Counselor
Assistant Professor
East Carolina University, Counselor and Adult Education Department
Greenville, NC

J. Scott Glass
Associate Professor
East Carolina University
Greenville, NC

About the Authors

Richard A. Lougy has been living and working in Sacramento, California, for the last 30 years, where he began his career as a middle school teacher. During that time, he also served as an elementary school counselor and later as a school psychologist. Before retiring in 2007, he oversaw mental health services for Head Start and Early Head Start programs in a large metropolitan school district in Northern California.

Richard currently runs a private practice specializing in ADHD and related disorders as well as being a mental health consultant for early head start programs and before and afterschool care programs for a large school district.

He has treated and worked with thousands of children with ADHD and their families throughout his career. In addition to coauthoring two books on ADHD—*ADHD: A Survival Guide for Parents and Teachers* (2002) and *Teaching Young Children With ADHD: Successful Strategies and Practical Interventions for PreK–3* (2007)—he has also written numerous articles on ADHD and regularly presents at state and national conferences. He lives in Lincoln, California, with his wife Linda.

Photo by Bill Mahon

Silvia L. DeRuvo is a special education resources development specialist with WestEd, a nonprofit agency that works with schools, districts, state agencies, and national policy makers in the areas of educational research, products, and programs. Her work focuses primarily on working with schools and teachers on effective research-based instructional practices that support the needs of students with disabilities within core content integrated classrooms. Prior to her work at WestEd, Silvia has been an elementary special educator for nearly 20 years and a teacher trainer at California State University, Sacramento.

Her experience in the classroom, as well as in state special education leadership, has given her vast experience in the area of special education practices and effective inclusion practices that support the needs of students with ADHD and other learning disabilities. She is a national speaker for the Bureau of Education and Research on Response to Intervention implementation practices and is a coauthor of *Teaching Young Children With ADHD: Successful Strategies and Practical Interventions for PreK–3*, a book on classroom strategies for students with ADHD, published in 2007. She is currently authoring a book on instructional strategies to support secondary students with ADHD that will be published in 2009.

Silvia received an MA in communicative disorders and holds credentials in multiple subjects, special education specialist communications handicapped, and resource specialist certification from California State University, Fresno. Silvia lives in Northern California with her husband, two children, a dog, and five cats.

 **David Rosenthal, MD,** is an adult, adolescent, and child psychiatrist in private practice in Boulder, Colorado, where he resides with his wife and son. He is an adjunct professor in the Graduate School of Social Work at the University of Denver, where he teaches courses on psychopharmacology.

David earned his medical degree at the University of Iowa School of Medicine in 1986 and completed his residency in adult psychiatry and fellowship training in child and adolescent psychiatry at the University of California, Davis, Medical Center.

He practiced psychiatry in various settings in California for many years and treated thousands of patients with ADHD, anxiety, and mood disorders before coauthoring two books on ADHD: *ADHD: A Survival Guide for Parents and Teachers* (2007) and *Teaching Young Children With ADHD: Successful Strategies and Practical Interventions for PreK–3* (2007). He also has written articles on ADHD and regularly speaks at state and national conferences on ADHD.

1 What Is Attention-Deficit/Hyperactivity Disorder (ADHD)?

A DHD is one of the most publicized and controversial psychiatric disorders in the United States and one of the most studied of all psychological disorders in children (Barkley, 1995). Although our knowledge of ADHD is still incomplete and the diagnosis remains controversial, it is important that in your role as a school counselor you have a clear understanding of the disorder and the potential effects it has on the students that you will work with. Much of the confusion that you will find comes from the fact that so many experts are involved and their opinions regarding the diagnosis and treatment of ADHD vary widely, resulting in uncertainty about the status of this disorder and whether it should or should not be treated and, if so, how (Lougy & Rosenthal, 2002). Despite the fact that the definition of ADHD has been a "highly changeable definition, creating confusion among practitioners and the public" (Robin, 1998, p. 13), you will find that the needs of these students, whatever the label or definition, remains the same. The need for understanding, support, acceptance, and positive esteem remains unchanged. As the school counselor, you may be the only avenue that can provide this much needed support in the school setting.

As a knowledgable expert on ADHD and on the needs of your students, you will find that you are equipped to run interference to provide students with these much needed supports. We hope that you will find yourself equipped not only to support students in navigating through their school year but provide them with the tools they need to become successful adults. To play this all important role, the school counselor must have a clear understanding of what ADHD is, how it is manifested in children and adolescents, and how to educate parents, school staff, and other support providers on these characteristics. Most importantly, a better understanding of this disorder will prepare you to better to understand, accept, and establish a positive rapport with the young clients with ADHD that you will work with.

Is ADHD a Mythical Disorder?

ADHD is not just a temporary state that a child will outgrow or a normal phase of childhood that will pass in time. It is not behaviors caused by parental failure to discipline the child or willfulness caused by bad temperament but a real disorder that can be confusing, heartbreaking, and nerve-wracking to the child and the family that surrounds them. Even though there are no outward signs that a handicap is present, ADHD, like other disabilities, can bring significant challenges to the child and his or her family (Barkley, 1995).

It is important to note that ADHD is not a mythical disorder recently fabricated by the American Psychiatric Association (APA) or pharmaceutical companies for personal gain, as suggested by some groups and writers. As Anastopoulos and Shelton (2001) note, "There is little justification for claiming that ADHD is merely a 'disorder of the 90s'" (p. 21). Descriptions of behaviors that are indicative of ADHD go back to the year 1902. The scientific community has researched the disorder for many years, both in the United States as well as in the international mental health community.

Theory Versus Scientific Fact

Some educators and parents can become confused when hearing that ADHD is "just a theory" by outspoken critics against the current trend in diagnosing children with ADHD. In popular usage, the concept of "a theory" often implies rather weakly supported thought. However, in science, the term theory is a much stronger term. In science, theories are proposed, then tested, and tentatively accepted or discarded. If attempts to falsify a theory fail, the theory is considered likely to be correct—but it is still called a theory (Comings, 2008).

The importance for correcting this misconception is that, if not changed, it can give ballast to those educators who see ADHD as a myth and educational accommodations as unfair. Most educators are aware today that ADHD is not a theory but a scientific fact. However, authorities on ADHD, like Dr. Robin (1998), write that the question "does ADHD really exist?"

surfaces regularly in the media in the United States. He also suggests that many educators are familiar with Thomas Armstrong, an outspoken critic of ADHD, who wrote *The Myth of the ADHD Child* (1995). Dr. Armstrong has credibility in the educational community because of his previous work—particularly multiple intelligence. Dr. Robin writes, after presenting a four-step response to Armstrong's arguments against the scientific validity of ADHD, that his book is disconcerting in that "there are sufficient half-truths, distortions, and inaccuracies in this book, which, if seriously adhered to, would hurt the plight of many youngsters who continue to need lifelong interventions for ADHD" (p. 44).

It is important that school counselors, before moving on, be ready to address any questions as to the scientific validity of ADHD. ADHD, as will be outlined in this chapter, has been studied and researched by the scientific community both in the United States and the international community and is today recognized as a neurobiological disorder by a number of medical associations: American Medical Association, American Psychiatric Association, and American Pediatric Association, to name but a few.

ADHD Is a Complex Set of Behaviors

Research has shown that a *complex set of behaviors* has been observed in children and adolescents identified with ADHD. There is general consensus by experts that both children and adolescents exhibit similar *core symptoms* (i.e., inattention, hyperactivity, impulsivity) to various degrees (Anastopoulos & Shelton, 2001; Barkley, 1995; Comings, 2001; Robin, 1998; Teeter, 1998). To a lesser degree, in addition to the core symptoms, children with ADHD also have primary difficulties in following rules and display tremendous variability in task performance (Barkley, 1997).

Although the core symptoms (inattention, hyperactivity, impulsivity) have been called the "holy trinity" of ADHD, Russell Barkley (1997) proposes that behavioral inhibition or poor regulation of behavior is the hallmark of ADHD. He writes that

> continuing to refer to this disorder as simply an attention deficit may be a gross understatement of what has become increasingly evident in contemporary research: ADHD represents a developmental disorder of behavioral inhibition that interferes with self-regulation and the organization of behavior toward the future. (p. 3)

As a consequence, affected children's behaviors tend to be unplanned, unreasoned, and emotional and seem to be lacking organization, purpose, and intent—which can and does adversely affect their academic performance, school productivity, family relationships, and social and emotional development.

DIAGNOSTIC CRITERIA

The APA's *Diagnostic and Statistical Manual of Mental Disorders (DSM-IV-TR;* (2000) notes that "the essential feature of Attention Deficit/Hyperactivity Disorder is a persistent pattern of inattention and/or hyperactivity-impulsivity that is more frequent and severe than is typically observed in individuals at a comparable level of development" (p. 85). To be diagnosed with ADHD, "some impairment from the symptoms must be present in a least two settings (e.g., at home and at school or work) [and] there must be clear evidence of interference with developmentally appropriate social, academic, or occupational functioning" (p. 85). If the behaviors are only seen in one setting, then the behavior is more likely a result of the environment rather than ADHD. The affected child must manifest persistent patterns of ADHD behaviors that are "more frequent and severe," unlike an unaffected child, who may show ADHD-like behaviors only at certain times. The *DSM-IV-TR* (2000) also notes that

> signs of the disorder may be minimal or absent when the person is under very strict control, is in a novel setting, is engaged in especially interesting activities, is in a one-on-one situation . . . or while the person experiences frequent rewards for appropriate behavior. (pp. 86–87)

The context-related variability of the disorder, where a child will manifest behaviors indicative of ADHD is one setting and not another, is often taken to mean that it isn't present (Anastopoulos & Shelton, 2001).

In a school setting, there are many environmental factors that can cause a child who may not have ADHD to exhibit ADHD-like behaviors. A lack of classroom structure and routine, unclear teacher expectations, lack of engaging lessons, and poor behavior management may create behaviors in otherwise normal children that may be misconstrued as ADHD. In these environments, children are unclear about behavioral, academic, and social expectations and, in the absence of clear expectations, find themselves lost, anxious, and out of control. This kind of environment, often accompanied by clutter, too much downtime, unstructured free time, and boring tasks will create a structural vacuum where children will create their own structure, often including attention-seeking behaviors, acting out behaviors, and uncontrolled movement around the classroom. This teacher may report these behaviors as ADHD like, but when investigating these behaviors further, the counselor or student study team (SST) team may find that these behaviors do not occur at home or in other educational settings because the parents or teachers provided clear behavioral, academic, and social expectations. In this case, it is the teaching environment that has caused the behaviors, not an ADHD disorder.

Manifestations of ADHD

ADHD is a disorder that is often misunderstood by teachers because of the many different manifestations of ADHD in children. Not all children present ADHD in the same manner or to the same degree, making it difficult for the classroom teacher to clearly identify the behaviors that truly are a manifestation of the disorder. The current diagnosis of ADHD is divided into four categories. The precise category that a child's diagnosis will fall under will depend on the component that is most representative of the child's behavior. The four subtypes of ADHD are as follows.

1. Combined Type (ADHD-C)

This diagnosis applies to children who present predominantly with inattention and hyperactivity but not significant impulsivity (*DSM-IV-TR*, 2000). These are fidgety children who have difficulty staying seated, struggle finishing classroom assignments, often lose assignments, are easily distracted by extraneous stimuli (like noises in the hallway), and often forget the daily routines without reminders.

2. Predominantly Inattentive Type (ADHD-I)

This diagnosis applies to children who present with inattention but neither hyperactivity nor impulsivity (*DSM-IV-TR*, 2000). These children are often seen as daydreamers or as underachievers and are inattentive and unfocused. Their distractibility is many times internalized and is not always recognized by teachers. These children also struggle with organizational skills and have difficulty finishing work.

3. Predominantly Hyperactive-Impulsive Type (ADHD-HI)

This diagnosis applies to children who present with hyperactivity and impulsivity that is maladaptive and inconsistent with their developmental level. These children do not usually present with inattention (*DSM-IV-TR*, 2000). This population of children typically has the most difficulties with schools and outside agencies (e.g., law enforcement or social services). In the classroom, these children seem to be constantly on the go, not seated, talking all the time, and are involved in behaviors that may not be safe or logical. Their high impulsivity often leads to problems on the playground and with peers.

4. Not Otherwise Specified (ADHD-NOS)

This diagnosis applies to "disorders with prominent symptoms of inattention or hyperactivity/impulsivity that do not meet the criteria for attention-deficit/hyperactivity disorder" (*DSM-IV-TR*, 2000). This population, typically adolescents and adults, still present some of the symptoms and are often diagnosed with either ADHD-NOS or *ADHD in partial remission*. Therefore, even though an adolescent or adult may no longer meet the criteria for a diagnosis of ADHD, she or he can still present functional impairment in school and work.

One remaining category sometimes referenced is *late-onset ADHD*, where all criteria are met except for onset prior to seven years of age (*DSM-IV-TR*, 2000, pp. 85–93). Often, the late-onset ADHD population presents similar patterns of psychiatric comorbidity (mood and anxiety disorders) and functional impairment (school problems, legal problems, driving problems) as the full ADHD population (Faraone et al., 2006). For these students, the symptoms may not become apparent until puberty when teacher demands and expectations in school require more focused attention, greater organization skill, and more independent study skills. Poor executive functioning, which may have always been present, does not become an issue until tasks that tax the executive functions become a part of the middle and high school experience. This change in demand for organization and multitasking and the need to develop and stick to a long-range plan makes the ADHD symptoms of inattention more apparent. Teachers and parents often report that around puberty they begin to see an increase in irritability, mood swings, and academic difficulties in their children later diagnosed with ADHD (Nadeau, Littman, & Quinn, 1999, p. 43).

PREVALENCE OF ADHD

ADHD is a disorder that affects 3% to 20% of the population, depending on the information source. Most experts accept a range of 3% to 7% as the percentage of the population diagnosed with ADHD (Vaughan &

Kratochvil, 2006). Findings of studies conducted in New Zealand, Canada, and Germany show an overall prevalence rate of 3% to 7%, similar to prevalence rates in the United States (Hoagwood, Jensen, Feil, Benedetto, & Bhatara, 2000). A report from the 2003 National Survey of Children's Health stated that approximately 4.4 million children ages 4 to 17 years in the United States had a history of ADHD diagnosis (Bukstein, 2006). The male to female ratio is 4:1 for the predominantly hyperactive type (ADHD-HI) and 2:1 for the predominantly inattentive type (ADHD-I). ADHD may be underidentified in girls (Sadiq, 2007). Girls have often been overlooked because they often lack the classic symptoms of hyperactivity and impulsivity. Typically, girls do not disrupt classes, but they have clinically meaningful levels of inattention and underachievement, related, in part, to poor self-esteem (Thurber, Heller, & Hinshaw, 2002). Affected girls often have more problems with focused or selective components of attention. In the classroom, they often appear sluggish and less accurate in information processing and struggle with memory retrieval problems. These girls have more anxiety, mood disorders, and are often seen as shy, withdrawn, reticent, or apprehensive (Nadeau, Littman, & Quinn, 1999, p. 46). These behaviors make them seem unengaged and uninterested in learning.

Reports have consistently identified three aspects of ADHD where there are significant gender-related differences (Reid et al., 2008).

- There is a difference in symptom patterns between boys and girls. Girls are generally less impulsive while boys present with more discipline problems.
- There is a difference in distribution of ADHD subtypes. Girls are more likely to have ADHD-I.
- There is a difference in associated conditions. Girls are less likely to have a learning disability and have less risk for depression, conduct disorder, and oppositional-defiant disorder (ODD) than boys with ADHD.

Over the last three decades, the number of children diagnosed with ADHD has been increasing. According to the U.S. National Ambulatory Medical Care Survey, the number of children who received a diagnosis of ADHD increased 250% from 1990 to 1998. Kelleher, McInerny, Gardner, Childs, and Wasserman (2000) reported that pediatricians identified ADHD in 9.2% of children in 1996 compared to 1.4% of children in 1979, an increase of 657%. Do these statistics represent an epidemic or a heightened awareness of the problem, or are there a variety of forces at work pushing this diagnosis?

We believe there are a variety of reasons for the increase in the number of children diagnosed with ADHD. First, there is a greater awareness by the general public about ADHD. Second, over the last decade, preschool and adolescent children are increasingly being identified with ADHD, whereas in the past, preschool children were rarely identified and professionals felt that most children outgrew ADHD by the time they had reached adolescence. Today, we know that both age groups can be appropriately identified and diagnosed. Third, because of insurance guidelines and restrictions, most children today are initially diagnosed with ADHD by pediatricians and family physicians, who may not have true expertise or knowledge of ADHD and proper diagnosis protocols. Because there are still very few *developmental* pediatricians, referrals to mental health specialist (such as a child and adolescent psychiatrist) are often made only if a child is presenting significant mental health concerns in addition to ADHD. Unfortunately, the consequence can be that a child may be misdiagnosed either because of limited time for assessment or because of inadequate expertise in ADHD by a pediatrician or family practitioner.

Robin (1998) offers other possibilities to explain the increase in the diagnosis of ADHD in the United States. He attributes the fast-paced, 15-second sound bite mentality of our culture, which tends to encourage ADHD-like behaviors, and the pressure in many middle-class circles for high achievement and the keen importance in finding good jobs. Because of these stresses, parents may look to a diagnosis such as ADHD and treatments such as medication to help their children climb the academic and economic ladder. Last, the recognition that ADHD is a life-span disorder has increased the number of adolescents and adults seeking evaluations (Robin, 1998, p. 28). Although overdiagnosis does occur, the reality is that most children will have a least one child with ADHD in their classroom (Barkley, 1990; Scahill & Schwab-Stone, 2000).

There is little debate that once ADHD has been diagnosed the disorder persists throughout childhood in the majority of cases (Teeter, 1998). Research literature and follow-up studies on ADHD show that prominent symptoms and impairment related to ADHD persist into adulthood approximately one-half the time (Biederman, Mick, & Faraone, 2006; Faraone et al., 2000). Current epidemiologic data estimate the prevalence of ADHD among adults at 5% in the United States population (Biederman, Seidman, et al., 2008). Also ADHD persists into adulthood in approximately 50% to 70% of affected adolescents (Barkley, Fischer, Edebrook, & Smallish, 1990; Weiss, Hechtman, Milroy, & Periman, 1985), with 90% to 95% of adolescents and adults with ADHD manifesting the inattention cluster of symptoms at least as a component of their disorder (Millstein, Wilens, Biederman, & Spencer, 1997). Presenting adults also typically have poor self-discipline, a short temper, difficulty establishing and keeping a routine, and difficulty thinking clearly (Wolf, & Wasserstein, 2001) as well as self-reporting lifelong effects and less satisfaction in key aspects of their lives because of their disorder (Biederman et al., 2006). Even though most ADHD adults show fairly good outcomes, Teeter (1998) references a report showing that 41% of adults had a comorbid disorder, including mood disorders, substance abuse, and antisocial behaviors.

These statistics point to the importance of early diagnosis and treatment as critical for minimizing the problems affected children will encounter in their academic activities and in their social interactions with peers and adults. Considering that ADHD is a treatable disorder and that educational and occupational deficits can often represent underattainment, early diagnosis and aggressive treatment, both medical and educational, is of critical importance. Studies have consistently documented that ADHD is associated with high levels of grade retention, need for tutoring, and placement in special classes (Biederman, Petty, et al., 2008). We can no longer assume that children with ADHD will no longer need educational accommodations to find success in school when they reach adolescence.

WHAT CAUSES ADHD?

According to the experts, ADHD is viewed as a neurodevelopmental disorder with strong evidence of family genetic risk factors that generally manifests in early childhood. The symptoms affect cognitive, academic, behavioral, emotional, and social functioning (Anastopoulos & Shelton, 2001; Barkley, 2000; Biederman et al., 1992; Comings, 2001).

There is increasing scientific awareness that ADHD is a heterogeneous disorder that carries a high risk of comorbidities, such as mood disorders and learning disabilities (Pastor & Reuben, 2002). The etiology of ADHD is unknown, although family studies of ADHD suggest a genetic basis for most forms of this disorder (Comings, 2001; Hechtman, 1996).

ADHD is often described as a *hypodopaminergic disorder* or a disorder of self-regulation, often called an *executive function dysfunction*. The most current studies suggest that ADHD symptoms are the result of diminished function of the prefrontal executive centers of the brain cortex, which are responsible for impulse control and sustained attention. In addition to ADHD behaviors, decreased activity of dopamine has been associated with increased risk for addiction (cigarette and substance abuse disorders). An imbalance in dopamine and norepinephrine, two primary neurotransmitter systems most directly involved in ADHD, contributes to the symptoms we see in ADHD (Sadiq, 2007). These two neurotransmitter systems work in concert with each other to control attention, inhibition, and motor planning. The medications used in the treatment of ADHD intervene by regulating norepinephrine and dopamine levels, thereby normalizing brain function and improving self-control (Barkley, 1990; Shekim, Javid, Dans, & Bylund, 1983).

Other areas of the brain thought to be involved in producing atypical functioning seen in the ADHD population are the frontostriatal complex, basil ganglia, and the right anterior frontal lobe (Sadiq, 2007).

PRIMARY SYMPTOMS AND COMMON IMPAIRMENTS

ADHD probably represents the extreme end of a spectrum of normal human traits that we all possess, and as with other human traits, ADHD undergoes developmental changes with maturity. If ADHD represents one end of a continuum of traits, then the problem with diagnosis lies in determining the boundary between the unaffected population and those with ADHD. We all have ADHD traits, and those diagnosed with ADHD may simply represent the extreme. This disorder can be viewed like other personal traits, such as reading ability, height, weight, or intelligence. Where one falls on the continuum determines whether one's trait is considered normal or abnormal. Children with ADHD differ in how much they inherit the traits in much the same way we all differ in how much we inherit height or intelligence. No two children inherit or present identical behaviors (Lougy & Rosenthal, 2002).

The primary symptoms associated with ADHD are *inattention, hyperactivity,* and *impulsivity.* The relative degree and pattern of these primary symptoms help clinicians better index this disorder for diagnostic purposes. These primary symptoms are briefly reviewed and profiled with a focus on those ADHD deficits that interfere in an affected student's academic and social-emotional development in the next section. Chapters 4 and 5 will discuss in more detail how these primary symptoms can impact a child's learning and behavior at school.

Inattention

Inattention is considered one of the core systems of ADHD (Anastopoulos & Shelton, 2001; Barkley, 1990; Teeter, 1998). Inattention typically refers to a complex set of processes. Sam and Michael Goldstein (1990) discussion of attention is helpful because it relates to tasks that are required at school and home.

1. A student who is having difficulty taking notes and paying attention to the teacher simultaneously would have a problem with *divided attention.*

2. A student who is described as a daydreamer, preoccupied with other activities instead of what is being talked about, would have a problem with *focused attention.*

3. A student who is distracted by outside noises, such as a door closing or a student walking down the aisle to the front of the classroom, would have a problem with *selective attention.*

4. A student who is unable to remain on a task long enough to sufficiently complete that task would have a problem with *sustained attention,* or *persistence.* An ADHD child's brain cannot delay the impulse to switch attention to other activities that catches the child's attention. This difficulty is often seen when a 20-minute assignment may take up to three hours to complete because of delays in sustained attention.

5. A student who is unable to wait for the next spelling word to be presented by the teacher would have a problem with *vigilance,* or *readiness to respond.*

Research suggests that deficits in attention are particularly evident under repetitive or boring conditions (Anastopoulos & Shelton, 2001; Barkley, 1997; Teeter, 1998), which could happen during classroom seatwork or tackling tedious homework. Furthermore, inattention may affect a child's ability to engage in free play for long periods of time or participate in organized sports, such as baseball (Pelham et al., 1990).

Difficulty maintaining effort is closely aligned with difficulty maintaining concentration and effort. The attention deficit is often verbalized by students as, "I'm bored." They become bored with most mundane, repetitive, and low-stimulation activities, especially schoolwork and instruction that is nonengaging. They will often seek out new and exciting experiences to keep their interest—having an "attentional bias toward novelty" (Robin, 1998, pp. 16–17). Sometimes this venture toward novelty can lead to high-risk behaviors in adolescence, such as sexual promiscuity, shoplifting, or drugs, to name but a few.

Often what stems from difficulties with inattention is the tendency to forget or lose important materials needed for school. They often will come to class unprepared, without paper, pen, pencil, or other necessary materials. The will often turn in assignments late or forget to turn them in at all. They often don't have the necessary books or information to do work in class or at home. Because they fail to write down homework assignments, they often have failing grades due to many missed assignments.

Inattention can also present itself at the opposite end of the spectrum—*hyperfocusing.* They tend to selectively focus on discrete things, having a white-hot focus on things that catch their interest. A child with ADHD can become so focused on an activity or assignment they are doing that holds their interest that they will fail to recognize that transitions in the classroom have occurred and do not hear the teacher instruct them to put their reading book away and get out their math book or go to recess.

During complex tasks, attention can be described as comprising of three processes related to self-regulation (Teeter, 1998), which can have a negative impact on schoolwork if not mastered.

1. Maintaining attention over time

2. Organizing and self-directing attention

3. Investing effort to attend to tasks

Children with ADHD are challenged by all three tasks, which can contribute to their challenges and often their failures in school, resulting in poor self-esteem and resultant behavior problems.

Hyperactivity

Although current research suggests that hyperactivity and impulsivity are different expressions of impaired behavioral inhibition (failure to inhibit the impulse for motor movement) (Robin, 1998), it is still helpful to discuss hyperactivity separately because it is the behavior teachers most associate with ADHD and where most ADHD assessment referrals are made.

When talking about ADHD with teachers, what first comes to their mind is the hyperactive child that wiggles around and disrupts their classroom. This hyperactive child is known by everyone and, some would say, pesters and annoys everyone they come in contact with. Every teacher in the school knows this child by name.

Hyperactivity is not just *high activity* but *disorganized and purposeless activity.* Hyperactivity refers to a range of excessive body movements ranging from restless, incessant fidgeting while seated, to frantic running around the room for no apparent reason. In the classroom, this may be seen as wiggling, rocking, and kneeling in the desk. It may also include chair tipping and rocking, leg bouncing, kicking, pencil tapping, humming, singing, noises, and any wide variety of constant body movement. Hyperactive children are often referred to as always "on the go" and "driven by a motor" (*DSM-IV-TR*, 2000). Younger affected children often jump, wiggle, squirm, run, and find it very hard to sit still or walk calmly from one place to another. They poke, grab, and touch things, especially where they shouldn't. Also these children have difficulty playing or engaging in leisure activities, are accident prone, can talk excessively, hang on the edge of a chair, or make excessive noises during quiet times. In a nutshell, hyperactive children have great difficulty managing their activity levels and are seemingly unable to stop without reminders (Lougy & Rosenthal, 2002).

The classic overactivity found in young children is often diminished or transformed by adolescence—transformed into "subjective feelings of restlessness" (Robin, 1998, p. 18). Even though an adolescent may not appear restless to a parent or teacher, they often feel that way, struggling to focus or control this enormous amount of pent-up energy. They manifest their restlessness in different ways from the younger child with ADHD. They will often fidget or show other signs of restlessness. Adolescents often will describe feeling confined if asked to sit in a classroom for too long or when seated at a desk to study for a long period of time. Teachers often will find nonstop talking (especially in girls) and badgering as two common manifestations of hyperactivity in adolescence. To reduce the pressure of the pent-up energy, some will aggressively provoke people around them to bring attention to a point and relieve a sense of their internal chaos (Alexander-Roberts, 1995). They can manifest great energy by channeling their energy into many activities, as well as sometimes getting as little as four to five hours of sleep at night. Their high energy can wear out their friends and family (Robin, 1998), and the teacher that works with this high level of energy daily can quickly become less tolerant of these behaviors in the classroom—resulting in many classroom removals and lost learning opportunities. The insistence and tradition that students are only seen as compliant or learning if sitting quietly in their seats creates a situation where students with ADHD are faced with an intolerable situation on a daily basis.

Impulsivity

Impulsivity can appear in many situations that can be frustrating to teachers, parents, and peers who interact with children with ADHD. Impulsivity is often seen as difficulty waiting one's turn, blurting out before thinking, and interrupting or intruding on others' time and space, behaviors that are essentially unacceptable in most classrooms. Impulsive students can often appear demanding, inflexible, and selfish. They often start things before the directions are completed, take things without thinking, and are often seen by others as difficult to be with for any length of time. They will butt into line to get ahead of someone or take another's turn in a game because they can't wait until their turn comes again. If they raise their hand in class rather than calling out, when called on, they won't know what to say. These students have trouble keeping friends and struggle with social skills because of their impulsive behaviors. They're not invited to parties or asked to participate in recess games or to be partners in group activities in the classroom (Lougy & Rosenthal, 2002), as they may be pushy, obstinate, and lack listening skills.

Adolescents can continue to demonstrate high impulsivity. *Behaviorally,* they often are driven by the moment and have a great difficulty with delayed gratification. They will do whatever pops into their mind without stopping to measure the consequence of their actions. They often opt for short-term gratification despite long-term pain for not completing a homework assignment or getting their chores done at home. They can be seen as irresponsible, selfish, immature, lazy, and outright rude. *Cognitively,* the impulsive adolescents rush through schoolwork, overlooking crucial details, making careless mistakes, and writing sloppily. *Emotionally,* impulsive adolescents can become easily frustrated, agitated, or moody and lose their temper quickly—sometimes accompanied by aggressive and verbal responses directed either at others or themselves (Robin, 1998).

In conclusion, the impulsive behaviors often lead to social rejection by peers, criticism from teachers, disciplinary action by the school, and exasperation and exhaustion from parents. After many years of experiencing rejection, punishment, and criticism, impulsive students can become oppositional and develop feelings of low self-esteem and victimization. They can also be challenged by comorbid (associated) disorders (learning disabilities, ODD, bipolar disorder, substance abuse, anxiety disorder, and depression) that can further impact their educational, social, and emotional development.

PREDOMINANTLY INATTENTIVE TYPE OF ADHD

Children with ADHD who present with the predominantly inattentive subtype may sit and quietly zone out; they are internally rather than externally distracted. They often are seen as underactive, foggy, and cognitively sluggish. Younger children who have the predominantly inattentive subtype are unlikely to be referred for professional evaluation of ADHD because they do not display more commonly recognized disruptive behavior (Barkley, 1995; Layey et al., 1998). They also have fewer problems than the child with ADHD-HI in making and keeping same-age friends or getting along with teachers and other adults. Consequently, early elementary children who do not manifest the hyperactive symptoms may be initially overlooked by the teacher, but they tend to have increased rates of academic problems as they advance in their schooling.

Inattentive behaviors manifested by these children are, however, chronic, pervasive, and problematic in their day-to-day activities. These children have difficulty attending to one thing because they often pay attention to everything! They may constantly scan the environment around them, distracted by all things except what needs their attention. Lacking the selection control to dispose of worthless information, they can often hear the lights buzz and the clock tick, making it difficult to determine which sounds should receive attention (Levine, 2002). Internally distracted, they may even look as if they are paying attention, but instead they are attending to the clothes the teacher is wearing or the glasses on the teacher's face. With all of this information activating their sensory perceptions, they will have a difficult time attending to the important aspects of an instructional period. With so much calling for their attention, they will usually choose to attend to something that they find immediately gratifying to help block out the other input that is calling for their attention.

As a result of their sluggish and half-attending to classroom instructions, they often make more mistakes than other children in following oral and written instructions. The student with ADHD-I is often challenged by sifting through the information given during instruction—having difficulty sorting out the relevant from the irrelevant (Barkley, 1995). Barkley (1995) references a study finding that children with ADHD-I also seem to struggle with tasks involving perceptual-motor speed or eye-hand coordination and have more trouble consistently recalling information they had learned as time passed.

Last, ADHD-I appears to affect boys and girls at nearly the same rate or prevalence. Dr. Thomas Phelan (1996) also places the ratio at 1:1, because the ratio diagnosed in adulthood seems equal for males and females (Alexander-Roberts, 1995). In contrast, ADHD-HI seems to occur nearly three times more often in boys than girls (Barkley, 1995).

SUMMARY

We have provided an in-depth overview of ADHD symptoms because the school counselor should understand the challenges they may encounter in working with these special students.

School counselors, school psychologist, and site administrators can play an important role in providing teachers with important information and guidance when teaching children with ADHD. As school professionals, you will find that ADHD can present significant challenges to children when asked to interface with the classroom and school environment and many school tasks. Because children with ADHD can often present with comorbid executive-function deficits (see Chapter 2), they can find the school environment to be more challenging than it is for unaffected students. Children with ADHD are asked to interface with a system that makes day-to-day school tasks nearly impossible for them. This can be especially frustrating and debilitating for students if their struggles are not understood or appreciated by their teacher, peers, or other school staff.

Melvin Levine (1993) so eloquently writes the following:

> The more we involve ourselves with disappointing children, the more we understand the risks they must take during childhood. . . . Their lives bear the scars of unjust accusation, chronic feelings of inadequacy, and shamelessly untapped talent. Understanding developmental variation, characterizing it without oversimplifying it, and intervening vigorously on behalf of developing humans experiencing inordinate failure—these are urgent needs. (p. 11)

Educating teachers and support school staff on this disorder is an "urgent need" that suggests both ethical and professional responsibility.

2 Impairments in Executive Functioning

This chapter, rather than focusing on *brain-based disciplines* (Denckla, 2007), will be looking at *executive function* (EF) as it relates to educational and behavioral performance (e.g., how delays in EF impacts planning, organization, study skills, and self-monitoring/checking skills). These terms are familiar to educators and are recognized from literature on learning disabilities.

WHY SPEND SO MUCH TIME ON EXECUTIVE FUNCTION?

I sometimes forget to turn in my homework. Am I stupid? My science teacher told the class that, I always had an excuse for doing poorly in his class because I had ADHD, but the rest of you don't. My teacher thinks I don't care and I use ADHD as an excuse.

—Ryan, eighth-grade student

First, the authors of this book feel strongly that teachers often do not understand or recognize the role that EF plays in ADHD behavior. Executive function deficit (EFD) is commonplace in people with ADHD and can play an important role both in academic and behavioral performance in school. Because deficits in EF are often present in children with ADHD, it is very important that educators understand this close association between ADHD and EF.

Second, educators, because of misinformation, can contribute to an atmosphere where children with ADHD are

> in danger of being emotionally traumatized by being called lazy, unmotivated, irresponsible, and other such words implying moral turpitude instead of neurodevelopmental disability or immaturity. Probably the greatest value in recognizing the neurodevelopmental/ neurocognitive domain called EF is to protect a sizable minority of children from being traumatized by what amounts to adult name-calling. (Denckla, 2007, p. 15)

WHAT IS EXECUTIVE FUNCTION?

The term *executive function* has been familiar to those who were trained in adult-oriented behavioral neurology for a number of years; however, in the 1980s, writers, such as Russell Barkley, were beginning to write about deficient executive function or its dysfunction as central to the meaning of the syndrome of ADHD (Barkley, 1997). Behavioral neurologists and neuropsychologists were captured by the term EF in the 1990s, and research continues to investigate the role of EF in ADHD and other neurodevelopmental disorders (Denckla, 2007).

ROLE OF EXECUTIVE FUNCTION AS RELATED TO ADHD

When reviewing the role of EF as related to ADHD, we have drawn primarily on the EF writings from two distinguished authorities on ADHD: Russell Barkley, PhD, and Thomas Brown, PhD. Barkley and Brown have researched and written extensively on this disorder, and both are internationally recognized experts on ADHD. We recommend that the reader refer to *Executive Function in Education: From Theory to Practice*, edited by Lynn Meltzer (2007), for a more complete introduction to EF as related to learning disabilities and other neurodevelopmental disorders.

SNAPSHOT OVERVIEW OF EXECUTIVE FUNCTION PROCESSES

Before reviewing Dr. Barkley's and Dr. Brown's ideas on EF, we will present a snapshot look at the primary EF processes (Meltzer & Krishnan, 2007, p. 74).

- Selecting relevant task goals
- Planning and organizing information and ideas

- Prioritizing and focusing on relevant themes rather than irrelevant details
- Initiating and sustaining activities
- Holding information in working memory
- Shifting strategies flexibly
- Inhibiting competing actions
- Self-monitoring, self-checking, and self-regulating behavior

Children with ADHD can exhibit weaknesses in many of these processes.

Deficit in Behavioral Inhibition

Russell Barkley

Barkley (1997) sees behavioral inhibition as the leading function in the chain of events provided by the EFs. Without proper functioning in behavioral inhibition, the EFs cannot occur without interference.

The term *EFs* refers to an individual's self-directed actions that are used to help that person regulate his or her behavior, that is, actions a person performs that help him or her exert more self-control and better reach his or her goals. EFs represent the internalization of behavior that helps us anticipate changes in the environment and events that lie ahead in time. It provides a sense of readiness, the ability to inhibit habitual responses, delaying gratification, and adjusting ones actions to changing conditions. It is, in some ways, a cognitive process that serves as a kind of supervisor or scheduler that helps one select a strategy to integrate information from different sources.

Affected children often do not exert self-control in reaching important goals, for example, putting off watching their favorite TV program so they can study and pass an important test the next day. Typical children will put off watching their favorite TV program to study if they know they have an exam the next day. On the other hand, children with ADHD are often driven by immediate gratification and will watch the TV program, test or no test; they do not take time to measure the consequences of their choices. Many children with ADHD show an aversion to delay, showing preferences for small and more immediate rewards compared to larger, delayed rewards (Doyle, 2006). For this reason, many classroom reward systems that include a long span of time before earning a reinforcer are not effective for children with ADHD. An unaffected child understands the need to reach the long-term goal of getting a good grade, which becomes more important than the immediate gratification of watching a favorite TV program.

COMPONENTS OF EXECUTIVE FUNCTION

Barkley's (1997) model suggests six components of EF. He considers four of the EFs to be covert, self-directed forms of behavior that yield information that is *internally* represented and exerts a controlling influence over the sixth component of the model—the *motor control and execution* system. Barkley suggests that in the ADHD population, these functions are impaired.

Component 1

Behavioral inhibition is the foundation of executive function—the reference point on which the next four components (numbers two through five) are dependent.

Component 2

Nonverbal working memory helps us guide behavior across time toward a goal—ability to maintain internal representations of sensory-motor information (holding events in mind, sense of time and imagination, hindsight and forethought).

These children will have a difficult time in a classroom without structural classroom support, such as an agenda and a regular classroom routine, because of their struggle with the sense of time. These children will often repeatedly ask when reading or recess will occur. Without a clear sense of time and what happens next, students cannot particularly guide their behavior toward a goal because their hindsight, what occurred yesterday at this time, and forethought, what might happen next, may be affected. These children seem to spin their wheels in the classroom but not get anything done because of this lack of clear structure. They are often touching things and moving about in an attempt to overcome their lack of ability to maintain internal representation of sensory motor information.

Component 3

Internalization of speech (verbal working memory) means for an individual to describe or reflect on an event before responding to it, central to development of rule-governed behavior.

These children often blurt out the answer without thinking or waiting for a prompt to answer. Part of this "rude" behavior comes from the children's own recognition that in a moment the thought will no longer be in their memory. They also do not maintain an internal dialogue that helps them reflect and think about consequences before acting on a thought. Their behaviors seem erratic, and they do not seem to learn from their mistakes. Regular classroom punishment is not very effective for children who struggle to develop these rule-governed behaviors because they do not use the process that most go through in thinking out, through internal conversation, the consequences and then developing alternate more appropriate behaviors. This cause-and-effect kind of thinking that is developed through the internalization of speech will have a significant effective on reading comprehension and the development of moral reasoning.

Component 4

Self-regulation of affect, motivation, and arousal means not reacting on emotion but evaluating events rationally, then reacting.

These children are a bundle of emotion and struggle significantly with emotional competence. According to Hooper and Umansky (2004), emotional competence has three parts including (1) emotional expression, (2) emotional understanding, and (3) emotional regulation. Affected children can struggle with emotional regulation and/or choosing an emotion that is appropriate for a particular situation. Asking them to project and determine how the other child might feel after an altercation may seem an impossible task—often leading caretakers to express that these children seldom say they are sorry. These children will struggle with the process steps necessary prior to reacting emotionally to a situation (Denham, 1998). Typically, developing children will first take notice of an emotion; second, they will consider what the emotion means to them; and finally, they'll choose an appropriate response. For ADHD-affected children who struggle with this area of EF, the process can fall apart at any of these three stages.

Component 5

Reconstitution is analysis, goal-directed behavior, flexibility, and promotion of problem solving and creativity.

These children, because of delays in EF, will often struggle with viewing new situations or new learning from a variety of perspectives. Analytical thinking, when not supported by graphic organizers to manage and organize thoughts and concepts, can be very difficult for children with ADHD. Without support to see how concepts, actions, and content are related and then internalized, goal-directed behavior becomes a struggle. These students seem to exhibit haphazard behaviors that do not seem to have any rhyme or reason because of their difficulties with structured problem-solving processes, often leading teachers and parents to comment that they "don't seem to learn from their mistakes."

Component 6

Behavioral inhibition, along with components two through five, exerts a controlling influence over the sixth component of Barkley's model, the *motor control and execution system.*

Studies measuring fine motor coordination, such as balance, pencil-and-paper mazes, and fine motor gestures, often find children with ADHD to be less coordinated in these areas (Mariani & Barkley, 1997). Handwriting is an example where flexibility and fluency of fine motor movement are built on complex arrangements of letters, words, and sentences. Speech is another example where assembly of complex fine motor sequences is important to articulate language. Children affected by ADHD are more likely than unaffected children to have speech problems (Barkley, 1997).

EXECUTIVE FUNCTIONS WORK TOGETHER IN VARIOUS COMBINATIONS

Thomas Brown

Like Barkley, Thomas Brown (2008) views attention as an "incredibly complex and multifaceted function of the mind," and "it plays a critical role in what we perceive, remember, think, feel, and do. And it is not just one isolated activity of the brain" (p. 12). Brown sees attention as "essentially a name for the integrated operation of the executive functions of the brain" (p. 12).

Brown (2008) views EFs as operating in an integrated way, and most people diagnosed with ADHD show impairment in some aspects of the six clusters he describes under the heading "Executive Functions Impaired in ADD Syndrome" in his article for *Attention* magazine (pp. 12–17).

Cluster 1: Organizing, Prioritizing, and Activating for Tasks

- Have difficulty getting started on tasks (completing homework assignments, doing chores or classroom assignments)
- Procrastinate, particularly with tasks not intrinsically interesting
- Have difficulty attending to what is most important to attend to (working on the history paper due the next day rather than playing Sudoku on the computer)
- Often fail to notice critical details (putting name at top of paper, noticing + versus – in a math quiz)
- Have difficulty figuring out how long a project will take or prioritizing and putting some items ahead of others

These children's problems with organization and prioritization are often the first to spark awareness that they may have ADHD. These are the children who have a backpack that can be referred to as "the black hole." This mess is because of the children's difficulty with identifying what is most important. The backpack contains important papers along with trash because the children are unable to determine which does and does not have importance. These children are not self-starters and will be seen sharpening their pencils, taking trips to the Kleenex box, trips to the restroom, and any number of other delay tactics to keep from beginning the task at hand. This procrastination accounts for many incomplete assignments and an inordinate amount of homework. These children cannot realistically determine how long a new task will take, usually underestimating the time needed, and they do not have the ability to prioritize tasks. Feeling overwhelmed and not having strategies to break the tasks into "doable parts," children will often give up before they even start. This, in addition to frequent negative feedback because of the failure to notice critical details, makes this area of weakness one that often makes children with ADHD failures in school.

Cluster 2: Focusing, Sustaining, and Shifting Attention to Tasks

- Have difficulty sustaining attention on a task long enough to complete it
- Have difficulty with selective attention (listening on the telephone or the words printed on a page)
- Have difficulty not being drawn away from a project by distractions (both internal and external)
- Have difficulty ignoring a myriad of thoughts, background noises, or room distractions (child walking down the aisle, pencil dropping on the floor)
- Are unable to stop focusing on one thing so they can redirect their attention to what is important ("locking on" to a sound on the radio when driving and not looking ahead or paying attention to the traffic)

These children pay attention to everything. Their lack of ability to attend to the important information leads them to become distracted by the noises in the hallway, the clothes the teacher is wearing, the seam of their socks on their toes, the conversation of students in the next row, the buzz of the lights, and the hum of the overhead projector fan, just to name a few. They are also bombarded by racing thoughts that compete with the important information that the teacher is sharing. These children have a very difficult time keeping their thoughts on a task long enough to complete it when there are so many other things vying for their attention.

Cluster 3: Regulating Alertness, Sustaining Effort, and Processing Speed

- Have difficulty keeping their eyes open when they have to sit still and be quiet, especially pronounced when the classroom teacher uses a lecture format to present information (Fatigue is suggested to be caused by chronic difficulties in sustaining attention.)
- Have difficulty getting a good night sleep (Affected children have difficulty settling into sleep even when they are tired and want to go to sleep.)
- Have difficulty completing certain school tasks because of slow processing speed (They will complain it takes them a particularly long time to read and write.)
- Have difficulty using a processing speed that is not too slow or too fast (When too fast, they often perform poorly because of carelessness and not attending to details.)

These children are often seen as the lazy and unmotivated students who have difficulty paying attention in class. They are often perceived as sleepy and bored. Although their fatigue may be organic, the lack of engaging instruction and the requirement to sit silently exacerbates the problem. These same students, even when alert and engaged, struggle with completing tasks because of much slower processing speeds, making assignment completion more difficult.

Cluster 4: Managing Frustration and Modulating Emotion

- Have "very low thresholds for frustration and chronic difficulty in regulating subjective emotional experiences and expression" (Brown, 1998, p. 15)
- Have disproportionate emotional reaction to frustration, short fuse, and low threshold for irritability
- Have emotions flooding their minds, leaving little room for any other thought
- Displace thoughts or feelings when in a high emotional state
- Are overly sensitive and react strongly to even minor slights or criticism
- Have chronic problems managing frustration and other emotions

These children are an emotional wreck. They are often perceived as having anger issues by their teacher and parents. They do not have the internal speech to regulate their behaviors or to determine appropriate emotional responses. They cannot identify the emotions of others while they are in a high emotional state. Because of the difficulties with emotional regulation, they do seem overly sensitive and very reactive. With this said, they do know what to do; they just have great difficulty doing it. These children often get labeled as "bad kids," when it really is a problem centered on developmental delays in self-regulation.

Cluster 5: Utilizing Working Memory and Accessing Recall

- Have difficulty with memory—impairments in working-memory, holding one bit of information active while working with another (remembering a telephone number you just heard so you can call the number)
- Have difficulty with communication (expressive and receptive aspects) because of working memory impairments
- Have difficulty retrieving information from long-term memory
- Have difficulty with proper functioning of working memory (important component in mastering many school academic core areas like reading, math, and written expression)

These children are significantly impacted by problems related to working memory. They frequently *forget* what they are supposed to do next, they *forget* to turn in their homework, and they *forget* important information while taking notes and taking tests. The difficulties with holding onto information in short-term memory keeps them from being able to affectively take notes and answer questions in class when they have to wait to respond or hold some of the information in working memory while they finish writing their notes. The difficulty with retrieving information from long-term memory has catastrophic impact when students are required to pass high-stakes tests to earn a high school diploma or graduate. The performance inconsistency that comes from not being able to retrieve what they know on command is extremely debilitating and causes many of the academic failures that these students experience. In addition to the academic effects of weaknesses in this area, the struggles with communication affecting their ability to express themselves appropriately and to understand the communication of others has serious implications on social skills development and competency.

Cluster 6: Monitoring and Self-Regulating Action

- Have difficulty slowing down and controlling their actions (act without much forethought, can be restless and hyperactive)

- Have difficulty "holding back" and getting started—"Most behaviors require the ability to act, to 'do it,' as well as the ability to inhibit, to refrain from acting" (Brown, 2008, p. 17).
- Have difficulty measuring or assessing the expectations to behave appropriately in social situations
- Have difficulty making thought-out responses rather than random decisions (series of guesses)
- Are excessively "focused on how others are reacting and are excessively self-conscious" (Brown, 1998, p. 17) (These children can be very shy, too inhibited, and resistant to group activities.)

These children can be the ones that teachers very quickly identify as having ADHD. Their constant restlessness and purposeless activity quickly catches the teacher's attention. These children may struggle with social situations because their lack of control keeps other children from wanting to play with them. They are emotionally volatile and struggle with empathetic thinking. They do not have a plan when dealing with others or their emotions making them a "loose cannon" on the playground. Academically, they lack a plan of action and rely on guesses and luck to do well in school. Without a specific plan or sequence of activities established, they struggle with getting started or completing work. Some students are so keenly aware of how they struggle with social skills that they are resistant to social situations and suffer from extreme social isolation.

Source: Attention Magazine, February 2008: Article by Thomas Brown, Executive Functions: Describing Six Aspects of a Complex Syndrome, pp. 12–17.

SUMMARY

Barkley and Brown both seem to suggest that EF is an "umbrella term," as suggested by one writer, that incorporates a collection of interrelated processes responsible for goal-directed and purposeful behavior (Meltzer, 2007, p. 79).

Barkley and Brown propose that in affected children, those self-monitoring and self-regulating tasks important for educational and social adjustment are often delayed or impaired because of neurodevelopmental delays in EF. Educational and positive peer relationships both depend to a large degree on proper functioning of EF. Table 2.1, Executive Function and Areas Affected (page 28), shows the areas of learning and social development associated with each cluster.

It should be noted, however, that when assessing EFs in preschool children, there is general debate about whether preschoolers do in fact display specific deficits in EF. One reason for the debate is that in very young children EFs may be inadequately developed. However, differences in EFs become more apparent with increasing age. Even though it is apparent that very young children can have substantial ADHD symptoms, it's possible that the executive model may not be applicable to this young age group (*Current ADHD Insights*, 2004). Also, there have been minimal studies looking at EF in the preschool population (Doyle, 2006).

An important contribution to academic and social-emotional adjustment in affected children depends to a large degree on providing academic accommodations and behavioral interventions to minimize core ADHD symptoms. As much as parents and teachers wish that the affected child be more self-directed, be a self-stopper, or be a self-starter, children with ADHD are challenged in all three behavior areas largely because of developmental delays in EFs. The school counselor can play a very important role by helping teachers and parents better understand this important contributor to the child's performance. Equally important, for the school counselor, is to advocate educational and behavioral accommodations in the school setting.

In conclusion, even though the authors recognize the very important role EF plays in affected children's school performance, we also recognize that many other factors can have impact on children's motivation and focusing. There is little debate that EF plays an important role in affected children's learning and behavior; however, we suggest that *important* is not *exclusive,* and we encourage the reader to be open to other factors that may be impacting affected children's educational performance. As we emphasize throughout the book, academic and behavioral interventions need to be tailored to each child, and a cookbook approach to student interventions often falls short in meeting a child's needs.

Table 2.1   Executive Function and Areas Affected

Cognitive Cluster	Executive Function	Areas Affected
Activation	Organizing Prioritizing Initiating Planning Strategizing Sequencing	Writing long-term projects Math word problems
Focus	Focusing Sustaining attention Shifting attention	Shifting between tasks Transitions Math word problems
Effort	Regulating alterness Sustaining speed Processing speed Pacing Managing time Resisting distraction	Reading comprehension Long-term projects
Emotion	Managing frustration Regulating emotions	Shifting between tasks Playing games Social skills Impulsivity
Memory	Utilizing working memory Accessing recall	Reading comprehension Math word problems
Action	Monitoring action Self-regulating action Inhibiting	Long-term projects Playing games Social skills Impulsivity

3 Treating Children With ADHD Fairly

In your role as the school counselor, you will often be called on to be an advocate for the students who need your services. As an effective advocate for students with ADHD, you must realize the significant differences between the concepts of *fair* and *equal*.

Fair and *Equal* Are Not the Same

Most people equate the words as having similar meanings, but *fair* and *equal* are not the same (Lavoie, 1996). While *fairness* is defined as providing what one needs, this is very different from the concept of *equal*, which involves providing each one with the same thing. You will often be defending the need for *fair* treatment of your young client because it is hard for some teachers and students to recognize these differences.

When teachers equate fair and equal, they will feel like they are cheating their other students when they are giving the student with ADHD the extra accommodations of time or a near point copy of the notes on the overhead. Some students may think it is not fair if one student gets special consideration when taking a test or having the homework modified, but once the differences between fair and equal are explained and demonstrated, children (especially young children) are very accepting of their classmates differences.

To objectively recognize the truth about fairness for children with ADHD, they need to be recognized as children with a disability. The disability of ADHD requires that these children be treated differently, but fairly. Just as a teacher would not refuse children in wheelchairs the use of a ramp or deny children with visual acuity weaknesses the use of their glasses because not all students have them, teachers must also provide the required accommodations or instructional adaptations necessary to help the children with ADHD become successful students.

THE SCHOOL COUNSELOR'S ROLE

As a school counselor, your role is to direct educators in respecting the dignity of these children, in practicing tolerance for who they are, and in providing them with classroom opportunities that allow them to be as successful as their peers (Lougy, DeRuvo, & Rosenthal, 2007). As the school counselor, you play an integral role in the success of children with ADHD.

Any successful client-counselor relationship needs to be built on these principles. It is only when this kind of trusting relationship has been developed can the counselor-client relationship produce effective change. If this trust relationship is compromised, the effectiveness of the counselor is jeopardized and often not reparable. Trust and confidence in the counselor are paramount in any therapeutic relationship. Finding the balance of providing confidential support to a child and still informing parents and teachers may be a difficult balance to find. Counselors will find that meeting the needs of the student with ADHD and providing support to teachers and parents requires extensive, effective communication skills in a collaborative approach.

THE SCHOOL COUNSELOR'S ROLE AS A CONSULTANT

The school counselor should see her or his role as that of a consultant. Three content areas are important to understand when reviewing the role that school counselors can play in the treatment of children with ADHD in a school setting.

1. Importance of ethical practice

2. School counselor as a consultant

3. Collaborative-consultation intervention model for school-based consultation

Importance of Ethical Practice and Behavior

The title *counselor* carries with it important expectations and responsibilities. When a parent, student, or teacher consults with a counselor, he or she, the client, has certain expectations.

1. Clients expect the counselor to be qualified to give advice in areas of concern brought to the counselor's attention. If not knowledgeable, the counselor will help the client find an appropriate referral for the help that is sought.

2. Clients expect the counselor to make decisions and recommendations with the client's best interest in mind.

3. Clients expect to be treated with respect.

4. Clients expect that communication between client and counselor is confidential.

Expectations

Expectations are what a person believes is likely to happen when entering a consultant role or responsibility. That is, what does the consultant expect to happen in a given situation? Expectations can be influenced by past experiences, preconceived notions, and overheard experiences of other consultants in similar situations, as well as openness and optimism about outcome. Professor Kampwirth (2006) cites one research paper finding significant relationship between elementary teachers' outcome expectancies and their later positive evaluation of the consultant "suggesting the need for establishing positive expectations as a foundation for beginning the consultation process" (p. 22) (Hughes, Grossman, & Barker, 1990).

Preferences

Preferences are what the consultant wants to happen, which may not always be what the consultant believes will happen. Teachers generally look to the collaboration method over the expert-oriented consultation. Kampwirth (2006) cites two studies that found that most teachers prefer either the collaborative model or independent solution generated rather than an expert model. One study that divided teachers as to experience and grade level found that elementary and inexperienced secondary teachers preferred a collaborative model, whereas experienced secondary teachers referred to work out the problem by themselves (Hughes & DeForest, 1993; Morrison, Walker, Wakefield, & Solberg, 1994). The authors experience is that parents, as well, often respond best to a collaborative model over the expert-oriented consultation, when dealing with school-based interventions.

Collaborative-Consultation Intervention Model for School-Based Consultation

During the last 20 years, there has been an increase in the use of the collaborative-consultation model in schools, as schools move away from isolation in teaching to a more collaborative structure that allows professionals to pool their talents and share decision making and problem solving.

Collaboration refers to a very specific kind of consultation that is defined as egalitarian and nonhierarchical. In a collaborative relationship, both parties have parity and they are working together because they have the desire to meet a common goal (Friend & Cook, 2003). Professor Kampwirth (2006) notes that in the collaborative-consultation model it is not necessary that any one person be the expert: "Collaborative consultation takes place between or among two or more people, with the role of expert shifting periodically among the participants" (p. 6).

As the needs of the situation change in regards to the successful education of children with ADHD, each person involved in the teams will bring specific areas of expertise to the table. For example, educators or parents can bring to the problem-solving team, such as the SST or individualized education program (IEP) team, their particular area of strength and knowledge, which in the end will produce the best possible outcome for the student. The parents may be the experts in discussing their child's temperament and strengths; the school counselor may be the expert in explaining how the child's family dynamics contributes to the student's social interactions at school; and the teachers generally knows best what instructional strategies or accommodations are the best fit for the child. The function of these teams is a perfect example of the core components of collaboration, which include the following:

- Parity among participants
- Mutual goals
- Shared responsibility and participation in decision making
- Sharing of resources
- Sharing accountability for outcomes (Friend & Cook, 2003)

The collaborative-consultation model extends beyond the problem-solving process to the implementation phase, where individuals on the team share accountability for outcomes. Each member will not play the same role, and in most cases, the primary person who will implement any recommendations will generally be the classroom teacher. Other school staff, parents, and the student can contribute by offering their areas of expertise (Kampwirth, 2006).

Kampwirth (2006) provides, through the acronym ACCEPT (see the following), an intervention model that acknowledges the consultant's, or school counselor's, philosophy about the consultee's or teacher's contributions. He writes that the acronym stands for the behaviors that are at the "heart of collaborative consultation" (pp. 7–8).

A *"Acknowledging* the consultee's predominant role in carrying out the planned interventions" (p. 7)

C *Commenting* positively on the efforts the consultee has made to try to solve the problem and the effort he or she is extending

C *Convincing* the consultee that he or she has good ideas to offer and that you will listen

E *"Expecting* that the consultee will take the lead in the development of ideas if encouraged to do so," and that the consultee will give equal weight to the consultant's ideas (p. 7)

P *"Pointing* out the possibilities for effective interventions based on the consultee's ideas" (p. 7), involves the consultant taking on the role of a *facilitator* of the consultee's ideas to help him or her think through both the pros and cons

T *Treating* the consultee as an equal partner—"One of the hallmarks of a collaborative model is that it brings adults together in an atmosphere of mutual respect. Both are equally expert, both need help from the other, and both give ideas and contribute to the final solutions" (p. 7).

In conclusion, the collaborative-consultation model supports and is a good fit with our multimodal approach to working with children affected by ADHD in a school setting. The school counselor as the consultant is pivotal in providing an avenue of positive and effective communication between the family and the school.

- Communication with other caretakers and professionals who work with the child
- Maintaining a spirit of collaboration with the teacher, parents, and child
- Maintaining a positive, optimistic stance that instills hope and empowers the teacher, parents, and child even when things are not going well

THE SCHOOL COUNSELOR'S ROLE IN HELPING TEACHERS BETTER UNDERSTAND

It is important that counselors help teachers better understand the scope of the educational and social challenges that accompany ADHD. An important role for school counselors is helping teachers to understand that classroom accommodations (e.g., preferential seating, modified homework, extended time for test taking) for a student with ADHD is not being unfair but is often a necessary educational intervention. Teachers generally are not familiar with the acute and long-term consequences of ADHD, as well as the potentially unsatisfactory outcomes for students who are not provided special accommodations. Without the knowledge and expertise provided by the school counselor, teachers can adversely affect a child's performance in school because of misinformation and misconceptions about ADHD.

EXPLAINING RISK FACTORS ON SCHOOL PERFORMANCE

Learning Difficulties

Note: see Chapter 4 for a more in-depth discussion on learning difficulties.

Many children with ADHD have associated learning problems with input, organization, memory, and output (Silver, 1992) that can impact their academic performance. Research has established that co-occurring learning challenges are the norm, not the exception, for many children with ADHD, leading to high levels of educational and employment deficits (Biederman, Petty, et al., 2008). Experts estimate that 10% to 40% of children with ADHD have associated learning disorders that meet the criteria for a specific learning disability (Batshaw, 2002). Typically, children with ADHD and learning disabilities exhibit overall academic underachievement, displaying the most difficulty with reading and written language. Affected children also have a high incidence of central auditory processing disorders and visual-motor functioning problems, which affects all aspects of classroom performance (Lougy, DeRuvo, & Rosenthal, 2007). Learning disabilities can exacerbate ADHD symptoms and, if not properly addressed, can contribute to some affected children presenting early onset mood and/or oppositional-defiant disorders (ODD) (Anastopoulos & Shelton, 2001).

In some cases, students with ADHD will not only have a learning disability but associated disorders, such as ODD, depression, and anxiety disorders, which can impact their performance in school. Students with impaired impulse control and/or a mood disorder will sometimes be labeled with ADHD and bipolar disorder (Findling, Arnold, Greenhill, Kratochvil, & McGough, 2007).

Children with ADHD can also be challenged by significant behavioral problems stemming from environmental stressors as well as poor impulse control, which can often lead to negative interactions with school staff and with peers. The constant cycle of negativity leads to social isolation and low self-image. In addition to social isolation at school, another factor that can complicate ADHD is a child's personal social situation (Blackman, 1999). Numerous studies have found that children with ADHD are rejected more often by their peer groups, sometimes within hours or days of entering a new peer group (Erhardt & Hinshaw, 1994). Unfortunately, children with ADHD often like their peers more than their peers like them. Evidence suggests that affected children may not be aware of this discrepancy (Diener & Milich, 1997). As children with ADHD enter adolescence, they participate less than their unaffected peers in social activities and spend less free time with friends and family (Biederman et al., 2006).

Although ADHD may not be primarily driven by environmental factors, sometimes counselors fail to recognize how this disorder can trigger severe family chaos, parental discord, abuse, and other psychosocial stressors that can ultimately impact a child's performance in school. Because child abuse has a higher-than-expected overlap (Endo, Sugiyama, & Someya, 2006; Rucklidge, Brown, Crawford, & Kaplan, 2006) for children with ADHD, counselors must be highly vigilant to the possibility that children, especially young children with ADHD, are at a greater risk for abuse.

Consequently, because of subsequent academic, behavioral, and environmental risk factors associated with ADHD, it is imperative that educators provide affected students the educational accommodations and adaptations they need. Unfortunately, the authors have experienced many adolescents, who after suffering years of academic failure, felt embittered that their disorder was not properly addressed by their teachers and counselors. Educators who equate fair and equal often disallow appropriate accommodations that can provide a level playing field for an affected student.

ENCOUNTERING TEACHERS WHO SEEM VERY RESISTANT TO ACCOMMODATIONS

A counselor sometimes will be faced with a teacher who because of professional or personal feelings is resistant to any suggestions around accommodations. Consequently, you may be asking yourself—what can a counselor do?

- It's important to remember that as a counselor you can only offer the opportunity for change; you cannot make it happen.
- Some teachers find it very difficult because of temperament or personal history to teach a child with ADHD—the teacher is a "bad fit."

and every effort should be made to make a class change, if possible, especially with younger children.

- Educating the teacher on ADHD can go a long way in helping the teacher be more sympathetic and understanding toward the affected child.
- Behavioral changes often stem more from the relationship between the counselor and teacher than from any reading material. The authors have found that when a counselor has established a positive and supportive relationship with the teacher, the teacher often is more open to making accommodations for the affected child.
- Teachers, like students, often want to be listened to, not criticized. Empathy can go a long way in breaking down barriers to change or understanding.
- It is an unreasonable expectation to think that a counselor can reach all teachers. Sadly, some teachers will never be receptive to the counselor's ideas or the affected child's disorder.

These suggestions, though not foolproof, often can help a counselor find more success in working with teachers who seem not to understand the affected student's educational and behavioral challenges.

THE SCHOOL COUNSELOR'S ROLE IN HELPING PARENTS BETTER UNDERSTAND

Educating parents about ADHD is also integral to helping them help their child find success in school. Parents need to better understand both the educational and social-emotional challenges that are presented to children with ADHD. They need to clearly understand and advocate for appropriate educational accommodations for their child. Parents, often like teachers, express that giving children special accommodations will only "give them excuses" and lower the academic standard or expectation for them. Parents need to understand that accommodations level the playing field and do not provide unfair advantage.

Effectively educating the parents can evoke a series of positive results. The parents will be able to better understand the challenges their child may experience in school and often feel less guilty over their child's behaviors.

In a section titled "Education and Counseling Work Together" of Thomas Phelan's (1996) book, he presents three important areas to cover with parents.

1. The No-Fault Idea

The *no-fault* ideas have two major implications. First, the parents don't need to crucify themselves with guilt about what they did to produce their child's bad behavior. The second implication is that ADHD wasn't the child's fault either.

2. The Symptom Rating Scale

It's important that the parents and child are educated on the basic symptoms of ADHD. Both parents and child need to know which symptoms they are going to have a harder time with and which ADHD traits are milder or nonexistent.

3. Self-Esteem Work

Like many of us, ADHD parents will distort or overemphasize the negative and forget what they do well. Parents will often need self-esteem work for themselves. They need to be reminded of all the things they do right for their child—reminding them of all the hard work they do on a daily basis just to keep the kid afloat. The counselor can play a very important role in assuring that the parents see their successes and not just their "failures."

THE COUNSELOR'S ROLE IN HELPING PARENTS TALK TO THEIR CHILD ABOUT ADHD

Parents, when first learning their child is diagnosed with ADHD, can go through a litany of emotions: anger, grief, and, hopefully with time, acceptance (Barkley, 1995). However, some parents will be so relieved on finding an explanation for their child's behaviors that they will jump for joy. Finally, they have been given a reason and explanation for their child's behaviors. No longer do they have to feel that they have somehow let their child down, been a bad parent, or at a loss when trying to explain their child's behaviors to relatives and school staff.

After accepting their child's diagnosis, the parents will often ask the counselor, "How do I talk with my child about this diagnosis?" This is an important question, and how it is addressed can make a big difference in a child's attitude toward the diagnosis. The authors have found the following hints helpful.

- Counselors should first recognize that parents will come to their office with a wide range of understanding about ADHD. If their knowledge is limited or distorted, it's important to take time to educate the parents about the disorder so they have accurate information when they speak with their child.

- The parents should choose a time and place that is private, quiet, and safe. The parents need to block off enough time for questions or for dealing with upset feelings. It's not a subject area that should be discussed quickly, on the spur of the moment, or in the car while driving to the grocery store. This meeting should be planned, and careful consideration should be made by the parents on what will and will not be discussed. Both parents should be present if possible, and the parents should be careful to assure that other siblings or family members are not present when they talk with their child—this is a meeting between the affected child and the parents!

- The counselor should provide specific words or ideas the parents can use when talking with their child. However, how much information parents should share will depend on the child's age and maturity. Very young children only need limited information. (e.g., "Bobby, you take this pill so you are able to pay better attention in class—just like Mommy wears glasses so she can see better," or "Dr. Roberts said this pill, like your bike brakes, will help you stop when you need to slow down," or "Sarah, you sometimes don't always listen because it's hard for you to pay attention. It's not your fault; that's why Dr. Roberts is helping Mommy and Daddy find ways to help you do better.") With an older child (authors suggest around nine years of age and older), the parents should be more direct and talk with their child about the diagnosis. Older children are more capable of understanding how the diagnosis can explain many of their challenges.

- The parents need to understand that their child may listen closely and ask many questions, may react negatively to what the parents are saying, or show no reaction at all when told of the diagnosis. A lot depends on the parent-child relationship, age of the child (adolescents can be thankful, argumentative, angry, or in denial; latency-age children often want to understand but find it difficult to comprehend except areas that are especially important to them), and—if the child was listening or *again* distracted—wanting the parents to stop so the child could get back to what he or she was doing.

- The parents should be encouraged to use examples where the diagnosis has impacted their child's behavior and academic performance rather than scientific explanations that can often be overwhelming (e.g., not remembering to do chores, forgetting to bring home important books from school, taking a long time to do home-work, getting quickly upset at school). The authors have found that older children often seek out scientific information on their own through the Internet when it becomes important to them to know.

- The parents need to know as the child matures they can introduce more information that is important in helping their child address academic and social challenges. The parents don't need to overload the child with everything they have learned in one or two meetings.

- The parents and counselor should consult with the doctor. When talking about medication, it's important to have the child's doctor involvement or recommendations. Medical doctors have both the knowledge and experience to help parents talk about medication with their child.

THE PARENT-CHILD RELATIONSHIP WITH REGARD TO THE SCHOOL

It is critical that an open and supportive relationship be established between the counselor and the parents. The parents need to feel the counselor is a fair and *neutral player* who has their child's best interest at heart. The counselor cannot be seen only as a school employee who will align with the school against the parent when things get difficult. Often it is hard for a counselor to question an administrator or a teacher's decision; however, if the counselor is professional and presents a case based on professional judgment, it *generally* is taken without the other parties feeling attacked or betrayed.

Parental and Family Assessment Is Important

When an open and trusting relationship is established, the counselor can assess the parents for areas of strength as well as personal stresses that may be contributing to the child's difficulties at school.

Three parental areas that are important to assess are as follows.

1. Possible mental health concerns (parental depression, alcoholism, anxiety disorders, and untreated ADHD)

2. Marital conflicts (divorce rate appears to be higher in families that have children with ADHD)

3. Parental understanding of ADHD as it relates to their child's school and home behaviors

Although it may be difficult for the school counselor to impact the mental health concerns or marital conflicts in the family, they can have a strong influence in the area of parent education when a strong trusting relationship has been established. The school counselor can help parents see the connections between difficult home behaviors and how they are related to the school experience. Improved understanding of ADHD at home creates a more positive outlook for the affected child, even at school.

Fairness Comes From Empathy and Understanding

It is often hard for educators to understand that children with ADHD can experience very high levels of stress in school. Everyday school activities that unaffected children can handle with moderate support and encouragement, the child with ADHD will struggle with on a daily basis.

The Teacher Doesn't Live With an ADHD-Affected Child

One reason it is sometimes difficult to convince educators that children with the *invisible disability* of ADHD are especially challenged in school is that they view ADHD conceptually rather than experientially. Unless educators live with a child or adult with ADHD, or know one closely through a relative or friend, they are often unable to relate to the affected child's difficulties in class without being educated on this disorder.

A Teacher Isn't Privy to the Parents-Child Conflicts

Educators often are not privy to the ongoing fights, tears, frustration, or feelings of discouragement around schoolwork that goes on daily in the homes of children with ADHD. Parents often fight over what to do to try to help their child be more successful in school. Parents can grow increasingly depressed over nightly battles around homework, calls from school over their child's bad behavior, and their child's progressive isolation and alienation from other classmates. Out of the continuing discord between child and parents, there seems to develop a distancing that can be very painful to both child and the parents. Parents in pain, knowing that few understand their feelings of loss, blame themselves. Parents can come to sense a loss of their bond with their child but may not be able to put it into words. They see only dark clouds on the horizon, with little faith or hope the clouds will pass.

School Can Make Healing Between Parent and Child More Difficult

Schools become that ever present outside stress that makes healing between child and parents more difficult. Once again, the telephone rings and

Mr. Smith, the school principal, is on the other end of the line. The parent takes a deep breath, heart missing a beat, and answers, "Yes, Mr. Smith; how can I help you?" Mr. Smith called about Bobby, the mother's eight-year-old son who has hit a child on the playground. He needed to be restrained and was taken to the office, and he has to be picked up. The mother now faces not just another humiliating experience of removing her child from school, but has to find a way to get off work *again,* to her bosses chagrin, to deal with a situation that to her seems hopeless. She is sure that taking him home and putting him in time-out is not the answer, but all the answers seem completely elusive to her right now. She again is faced with dealing with her upset child who again sees himself as disappointing and upsetting his mother.

Parents of Affected Children Often Hate to Hear From Their Child's School

Unfortunately, calls from school generally come not to tell the parent what a great day their child had but to report an altercation with a teacher or child or some other infraction of a school rule. Parents of affected children usually hate to hear from their child's school. They may attempt to avoid contact with the school altogether, refusing to answer the phone, or not returning phone calls.

Teachers need to try to understand and not dismiss parents' feelings of alienation and perception of a lack of sympathy from educators toward their child's struggles in school. Often parents' anger toward a teacher or principal comes from their perception that the teacher and principal don't recognize or acknowledge their hard work or their child's struggles because of the disorder. They feel that educators often see their advocating for accommodations as an excuse and not a needed intervention so their child can be more successful in school.

THE EMPATHIC EDUCATOR

A caring, open, receptive, and empathic educator will find alternative ways to teach that can help affected children be successful in school and meet their potential.

Important Principles That Guide the Empathic Educator

- This educator accepts that being fair is not the same as being equal.
- This educator understands the concepts of universal access and universal design for learning.

- This educator has the innate ability to adapt and support teaching strategies to meet the needs of the student.
- This educator clearly understands the fairness principle and does not view adapting strategies as cheating or unfair.

THIS HIDDEN DISABILITY DOES NOT KEEP THE CHILD FROM SUCCEEDING

It is important to emphasize that when children with ADHD enter a classroom, even though they can be significantly challenged and challenging, they *can* be successful. We can look at some of the successful people who have struggled with ADHD and learning disabilities and yet have proven themselves successful in the world. Henry Winkler, Tom Cruise, Bill Hewlett, Bill Gates, Bruce Jenner, and Charles Schwab have all struggled with learning issues and are some the most successful people in our country. The hidden disability did not keep them from attaining their goals.

ROAD MAP FOR ASSURING FAIRNESS

The road map for assuring fairness has been drawn by others before us. Students with ADHD are eligible for special provisions through federal legislative protections for children with disabilities. It is important to understand that the provision for accommodations is generally available for affected children who demonstrate significant impairment in school because of their disorder. Schools are required under law to avoid discrimination and to provide specially designed academic instruction, if needed, for children with ADHD.

We also discuss important road maps for assuring greater success when working with affected children.

The Differentiated Classroom

Because students with ADHD will often present delays in both behavioral and academic performance, the importance of providing a differentiated classroom environment cannot be overstated.

In the differentiated classroom, teachers recognize that students vary in the amount of background knowledge they have, their readiness to learn, their language skills, their learning preferences, their interests, and last, their maturity.

Affected children often will have developmental delays in maturation, which can impact their social relationships and academic readiness (see Table 3.1, Typical Developmental Profile, for an overview of the developmental profile from middle childhood through adolescence).

Table 3.1   Typical Developmental Profile

An overview of typical developmental milestones in children can be your guidepost when comparing children with ADHD to unaffected children. As you will read, children with ADHD often are challenged by and delayed in mastering many of the following stages of development.

Phyllis Teeter (1998, pp. 110–149, 201–238) outlines developmental stages under the following categories for both middle childhood and adolescents.

Middle Childhood Stage (6 to 12 years of age)

The middle childhood stage of development is characterized by higher expectations for self-control, cooperation, compliance, and independence in the home, in the classroom, and in social situations. However, it is important to recognize that these developmental domains should be viewed as interdependent with child factors, such as temperament, attention, and self-control, and compliance, interacting with environmental factors, such as home environment, teacher relationships, expectations, and demands put on the child (Teeter, 1998).

Initiative and Self-Worth

- Are aware of their own social acceptability and competence
- Compare themselves to their peers
- Are realistic in terms of their assessment of their own performance
- View success as a function of the their ability

Self-Regulation and Self-Control

- Are more internal in their thinking
- Are more adept at controlling impulsive thoughts or actions
- Begin to anticipate the consequences of their actions and change their behaviors accordingly
- Are less aggressive and selfish in their actions
- Are more aware of society's expectations
- Have an increase in their ability to problem solve because of speech and language development

Cognitive Development

- Have major developmental changes in *conservation* (notion that properties don't change despite changes in size or shape), *classification* (ability to group objects into categories, discern differences and similarities between objects), and *memory*
- Become aware of themselves as learners and knowers, can use and evaluate strategies to learn, and develop strategies for remembering
- Have rapid vocabulary and linguistic skills development
- Have an increase in memory capacity
- Imitate organizational strategies when instructed to remember more information–use rehearsal strategies to aid in remembering
- Have rapid development of attention controls (more focused)

(Continued)

Table 3.1 (Continued)

Emotional Development

- Become adept at regulating their emotional reactions to events and situations
- Become more aware of their feelings and the rules for expressing them

Socialization and Peer Interactions

- Develop a sense that they are a part or function of their social group membership ("I am a sixth-grade student at Edison School.")
- Develop a sense of what others are thinking and feeling and change their ways in consideration of another's feelings
- Begin to strengthen their feelings of empathy
- Change friendship patterns—develop friends on the basis of intimacy and friendship
- Have an increased importance on friendships for learning problem-solving skills
- Have a rigid adherence to rules
- Behave in ways that are consistent with parental values

School Adjustment

- Develop academic self-esteem and feelings of competence when successful in school
- View school as an important environment for self-efficacy
- Develop academic competence in reading, mathematics, writing, and speaking

Adolescent Stage (12 to 20 years of age)

The age span for adolescence typically ranges from 12 to 20 years of age, with 12 years generally viewed as the approximation of the beginning of adolescence. Even for unaffected children, adolescence can be a challenging time. Successful adjustment to adolescence is often determined by the degree of success in handling middle childhood development. Consequently, early interventions and support at earlier stages of development can help alleviate the problems facing teens. The fact that unaffected teens find the adolescent stage to be one of great turmoil only adds to the importance of helping adolescents with ADHD through this stage of development (Teeter, 1998).

Physical and Sexual Maturation

- Experience rapid changes in sexual characteristics
- Show a great deal of variability as to when physical changes occur
- Variability of age onset of physical changes can effect social-emotional adjustment
- Become profoundly preoccupied with sex
- Sexual activity is affected by parenting style and family cohesion

Cognitive-Intellectual Development

- Advent of formal operational thinking (abstract thinking, hypothesis building)
- Analyze moral dilemmas and understand some solutions are often in the gray area (not necessarily right or wrong answers)
- Become aware of the role they play in their own learning (analyze their own performance, predict ahead of time how they will do, and change learning strategies to improve the outcome)
- Become egocentric—believing everyone is looking or talking about them or the belief that they are unique ("I am the only one who feels this way.")
- Underestimate their own vulnerability and potential risks
- Have an increase in the internal value of self-control

Psychosocial Development and Self-Identity

- Develop personal or self-identity
- Engage in a considerable amount of self-watching or self-evaluation
- Emotions and body image are important facets in the perception of self
- Have strained parent-teen relationships
- Rank freedom and friendships as the most important values
- Put great importance on status within the peer groups

Teachers must respond to all these specific needs with a variety of instructional strategies. Teachers adjust their instructional strategies in the following areas: content, process, and product (Gregory & Chapman, 2007; Tomlinson, 2000, 2001).

Content

The content of instruction is the standard or curriculum that is being taught. Teachers who differentiate in the area of *content* provide multiple examples of how students may meet one objective or standard, highlight the critical features that support meeting the objective, and provide the supporting background knowledge so that students can relate the situation to their experiences.

Process

How the teacher differentiates during instruction to meet the specific needs of students is referred to as *process*. Teachers who differentiate in the instructional process provide information in multimedia formats with numerous supported opportunities for practice, and they employ strategies that will engage all learners, including students with ADHD.

Outcome or Product

The *outcome* or *product* for the differentiated classroom allows flexible models and variations of skill performance as well as numerous opportunities to demonstrate skills to show that students have met the objective. Teachers who differentiate in outcome or product have the flexibility to create diverse assignments within the larger curriculum goal (Lougy, DeRuvo, & Rosenthal, 2007; Smutney & von Fremd, 2004).

Resistance to Providing a Differentiated Classroom

Unfortunately, teachers, when working with children with ADHD, often don't provide an engaging educational environment where affected children can be more successful. The authors have heard many reasons why alternative learning models or classroom settings are not used. Here are a few reasons.

- "If I use a different method of teaching, those students with ADHD will just get out of control."
- "If I allow the students to talk to each other they will get even more off task."
- "I won't be able to manage the classroom if students get to talk and interact with each other."
- "It will get too noisy."
- "I won't be able to keep those kids with ADHD on task."
- "Those kids with ADHD are lazy and will just let everyone else in their group do the work."

The differentiated classroom will look different from the traditional teacher-as-the-information-provider classroom. In a differentiated classroom students are engaged in learning through discussion with peers and interaction with the content utilizing a variety of modalities. Students with ADHD find success in these classrooms where they have an opportunity to interact with their peers and the content in a variety of ways.

Teachers who are reluctant to differentiate instruction may also be reluctant to implement accommodations within their daily classroom instruction for many of the following reasons.

- "He is using his ADHD diagnosis as an excuse."
- "She is not motivated, why should I reward her with less work."
- "It would be unfair to the other students to let my student with ADHD have extra time on a test."

- "If I make exceptions for my ADHD-affected students, then the other students will want the same."
- "I have 36 students in my classroom. I don't have time to make special arrangements for the ones with ADHD."

These reasons may sound familiar to you or reflect in part your own feelings in regards to students with ADHD. It is understandable that educators often are in a quandary trying to tease out enabling from fair accommodations. No responsible educator wants to reinforce manipulative or noncompliant behaviors by a student. It is not easy separating when affected students are "just being lazy" and when, because of high distractibility and delays in attention, they are overwhelmed and shutting down. We provide guidelines in Chapters 4 and 5 that will assist the counselor in distinguishing intentional manipulative behaviors from behaviors primarily triggered by ADHD symptoms.

Consulting With Teachers on the Importance of Accommodations

It is important when counseling or consulting with teachers about accommodations for students with ADHD that you cover three areas:

- Most students with ADHD can be more successful with only minor classroom accommodations.
- Accommodations for students with ADHD who demonstrate significant impairment in school are protected under civil rights legislation that educators cannot ignore or dismiss.
- An educator's *opinion* as to the accuracy of a child's diagnosis cannot be used to deny an affected student fair and appropriate accommodations under a Section 504 Plan or IEP.

Often, therefore, training on ADHD from a school counselor, school psychologist, or outside consultant is required for teaching staff. It is very important that school administrators be involved in the training so they understand the importance of their role in providing both the affected child and the classroom teacher with additional support when necessary.

Making Appropriate Educational Accommodations

You will read some appropriate interventions that address federal legislation protections when working with children with special needs. Understanding these processes will allow you as the counselor to educate the staff and parents that you work with.

Most students with ADHD do not need special education intervention but rather classroom and instruction accommodations to support their learning needs. It is important to understand the interventions that are available that often prevent the need for special education intervention: Response to Intervention, Section 504 Plan, and the Behavior Support Plan are processes that support both the academic and behavioral needs of students with ADHD.

Prevention and Intervention Prior to Referral to Special Education

Response to Intervention

Response to intervention (RTI) is the practice of providing high-quality instruction and intervention matched to student need, which sounds much like differentiation, but it involves more intentional and frequent progress monitoring and child responses to make important educational decisions (Batsche et al., 2005). RTI is a process described in the Individuals with Disabilities Education Act of 2004 (IDEA) for identifying students with learning disabilities. In an RTI model, all at-risk students are provided interventions early on, which research shows prevents some students from subsequently needing special education services. To qualify as learning disabled under this model, a child would "fail to respond" to intensive interventions provided before a referral to special education. The lack of response to the interventions becomes part of the process in the identification of a learning disability rather than a discrepancy between cognitive skills and academic achievement. This model seems to hold promise for those students who would benefit from early intervention services rather than having to wait until a significant discrepancy between ability and achievement appears.

Children with ADHD are affected negatively in the classroom because of a diminished capacity to maintain attention, which can impair their ability to focus on basic curriculum development during the primary grades. The consequence, as they move up in grades, is that they may develop gaps in their learning. The RTI models are intended to prevent such gaps from widening and to create a situation where the child will not need special education services. Without early intervention, these gaps become especially problematic in upper grades, where mastery or proficiency in basic curriculum is essential for academic success. When proficiency is poor, children with learning disabilities often feel like failures, and they are at risk for "giving up" during adolescence. They are at especially high risk for dropping out of school or not graduating under these conditions. Although medications may clearly ameliorate some of the core symptoms of ADHD, there are no medications that specifically target learning disabilities. There are, however, a wide variety of educational techniques and strategies that can be implemented to develop, strengthen, or compensate for weaknesses associated with many kinds of learning disabilities (Lougy, DeRuvo, & Rosenthal, 2007; Lougy & Rosenthal, 2002).

One study reported that there is some uncertainty as to the effects of stimulant medications on some domains of EF. Stimulant medications seem to help the EF domains of sustained attention and verbal learning, but stimulant treatment does not seem to have an effect on interference control and processing speed. The weakest effect of stimulant medication was in organization/planning. The authors suggest that the results of this study may "begin to explain the apparent dissociation between stimulant-associated improvement in core systems of ADHD and academic performance" (Biederman, Seidman, et al., 2008, p. 1154). Consequently, this study would suggest that many affected children often will need both psychoeducational and pharmocological interventions to find maximum support.

In recognition of the fact that children with ADHD often will have an associated learning disability, RTI intervention and prevention structures can serve to address the challenges often faced by students with ADHD in the classroom.

Behavior Support Plan (BSP) and Behavior Intervention Plans (BIP)

Many collaborative discussions involving students with ADHD revolve around behavioral issues. As a school counselor you may have an integral role in supporting the development of positive appropriate behaviors in your clients who have ADHD. Chapter 5 is dedicated to your specific role and responsibilities in the development of appropriate school behaviors for affected children. To assure that students with ADHD are not inappropriately labeled as having behavior disorders, again, it is important to be aware of prevention and intervention processes that will support the positive development of school behaviors for any child.

In addition to academic intervention, RTI also has a behavior component. Schools that adopt an RTI approach develop schoolwide positive behavior supports. This schoolwide consistent behavior structure will support the needs of most students. In this type of school climate, expectations are clear, consequences are fair, and the entire school staff supports a philosophy of positive behavior change rather than a punitive-punishment-based system. In this preventive approach, behavior is monitored for those students who struggle with these behavioral expectations. For these students, a secondary intervention may be necessary.

Behavior Support Plan

The school counselor may play an integral role in providing direct, targeted support to develop appropriate behaviors within this system. When data reveal that even a secondary intervention may not have been successful, a problem-solving team may develop a BSP. This plan is created to help children develop replacement behaviors for the ones that are causing them trouble. This plan involves effective collaboration and support by all parties involved in the education of the children.

Behavior Intervention Plan

If the BSP is not successful, it may be appropriate to evaluate the child for further emotional disturbance or other handicapping conditions. If children in special education continue to struggle with behavior despite special education support, a qualified team will perform a functional behavior analysis (FBA) and develop a BIP. Although this plan is developed with the expertise of a school psychologist and other professionals, the school counselor will often play an integral role in the implementation of the plan. This plan is designed for those students who already have an IEP and need intensive intervention to develop appropriate replacement behaviors.

Section 504 Plan

Children who have a diagnosis of ADHD but do not require specially designed academic instruction in special education may be entitled to accommodations and modifications under Section 504 of the Rehabilitation Act of 1973. It is important to keep in mind that not all children with ADHD are in fact in need of accommodations because, according to the law, the disorder must "substantially limit a major life activity, including . . . learning" (Section 504, 34 C.F.R. § 104.3 [i][1][ii]).

If the ADHD does limit a child's ability to learn and be successful in school, this civil rights legislation allows for accommodations. These accommodations provide children with ADHD an

> equal opportunity to obtain the same results, to gain the same benefit or to reach the same level of achievement. These aids or benefits are not required to produce the identical result, or level of achievement for both students with disabilities and those without. (Section 504, 34, C.F.R. § 104.33 [b] [1])

This broad civil rights law protects the rights of individuals with handicaps in programs that receive federal financial assistance and ensures that any person with a disability has the same rights and opportunities that his or her nondisabled peers have. A Section 504 plan is not a special education document, and it is not the responsibility of the special education staff at the site, although special educators are often called on to provide suggestions and support for the 504 Plan. They may also be involved in providing some of the accommodations that require a separate place to work or extra time for assignments (Lougy, DeRuvo, & Rosenthal, 2007). Accommodations allowed by the 504 Plan are permissible during daily classwork and for all school, district, and statewide assessments.

The authors would be remiss in not reporting that some advocates for affected children will argue that some school districts flaunt violations of the 504 law without suffering any consequences. They point out that the 504 law is relatively toothless because, although it is illegal to not accommodate, there is no penalty within the law for failing to accommodate. So they feel it is not the best protection when an affected student is being significantly challenged in school; rather, they advocate that under such circumstances, the best protection is to have the student be classified under IEP protection—such as other health impaired.

However, the authors experience is that when valued and properly implemented by schools, a 504 Plan will meet the educational needs for the vast majority of children significantly handicapped by their disorder.

Other Health Impaired

Although there are comorbid learning disabilities that often affect children diagnosed with ADHD, not all children who have ADHD who are tested qualify for special education services under the label of "specific learning disability." A child who is diagnosed with ADHD and is significantly impacted in all academic areas may qualify for special education services under the federal handicapping condition of other health impaired. This is not a common designation for most students who are only mildly affected by ADHD and is usually reserved for those children who do not respond to medication and behavioral therapy and need extra daily instructional support through special education services provided by the school in an IEP to successfully make educational progress (Lougy, DeRuvo, & Rosenthal, 2007).

Summary

As a school counselor it is your role to help educators understand that instructional accommodations and classroom adaptations support the learning of children with ADHD. Once this is understood, student success, motivation, and subsequent self-esteem will improve. When the unique qualities and gifts that these children present are clearly understood, classroom success is definitely attainable. We hope that the strategies you will find in the following chapters will help counselors guide teachers and other school staff in working more effectively with children with ADHD.

Treating children with ADHD fairly means complying with the law and assuring that these children are provided the necessary accommodations and instructional strategies that will help them become successful in school. Teachers, school administrators, school psychologist, and school counselors can help create a positive school climate that assures that children with ADHD receive fair treatment and find success every school day.

4 Classroom Strategies

A Recipe for Student Success

Silvia L. DeRuvo

Although children with ADHD often spend an inordinate amount of time doing schoolwork, this is usually not reflected in their grades. Although many of these students struggle because of accompanying learning disabilities, many of them (60% to 90%) do not (Stein, Efron, Schiff, & Glanzman, 2002).

The invisible and misunderstood disability of ADHD is often not recognized by the classroom teacher or other professionals who may work with the child, bringing the child to the attention of the school counselor. This lack of recognition often leads to misunderstanding, creating a shadow of negativity that falls over every single day of school for affected children. When teachers recognize that these children are not willful in their inability to attend, follow directions, or complete the myriad of assignments in a given day, will the teachers find the desire to change the way they teach to help these students find more success in school? Without the intervention of the school counselor, teachers will continue in the status quo, often falling back into the default mode of instruction, which relies heavily on the attentional skills and ability to listen and copy lecture notes.

In the age of accountability, where high-stakes testing determines students' ability to graduate and live above the poverty level, it is the vital intervention of the school counselor that can prevent students with ADHD from falling through the cracks.

THE SCHOOL COUNSELOR'S ROLE IN INCITING CHANGE

Change is difficult. Change is uncomfortable. No one likes to go through the change process. We are creatures of comfort and like to keep things as comfortable as possible. Going outside the comfort zone usually takes some pushing and prodding. As a school counselor, you may find yourself in the unpopular position of pushing people to change. We know from Vygotsky's (1978) research on teaching that learning occurs within the zone of *proximal distance,* and teachers use this method whenever they present content and tasks that are just outside of the children's current knowledge or skill level. This same strategy will have to be employed by the school counselor to incite the change needed in current instructional practices to meet the needs of students with ADHD. Change is inevitable because accountability has brought classrooms and teachers to the place where new practices must be embraced. But how can school counselors make an inroad into the classroom to provide the classroom teacher the necessary support to meet the needs of those children with ADHD, who are most often left behind?

Consulting and Support

The school counselor has the unique role of being sought out as an expert in a consultative manner when teachers are struggling with specific students. This process involves a *problem-solving team.* The team looks at a specific child and attempts to address the following questions. What is the problem? Why is it happening? And what is the solution (Tilly, 2008)? A counselor is an essential part of this important team.

When teachers need help and come to the problem-solving team for support, it creates the perfect consulting opportunity for the school counselor. The counselor helps the teacher identify why the problem is occurring and what can be done to alleviate the problem. Although the school counselor may not be the expert in instruction and instructional strategies, this chapter attempts to provide counselors with some tools that enable them to support teachers in a consultative manner. Though this chapter is by far not a comprehensive review of all the successful research-based instructional strategies available, it will highlight the most commonly used and those that have proven through research to be the most successful in increasing student learning. Although this research was not specifically geared toward students with ADHD, the effective instructional strategies covered in this chapter will support the specific learning needs of children with ADHD.

RECOGNIZING THE ACADEMIC CHALLENGES

Although the actions of children with ADHD are often referred to as lazy, unmotivated, or disorganized, the consequences of academic challenges often outweigh the lack of self-esteem that these terms can generate. Students with ADHD struggle with school. Each and every day brings before them challenges that no one else experiences. Each day can bring anxiety and feelings of defeat when their disability and need for specific accommodations and academic strategies are not recognized. In many ways, they are being asked to learn with "half an eye and half an ear" (Denckla, 2007).

As mentioned in Chapter 3, school challenges can impact children not only during the school day but can impact a parent-child relationship at home. Affected children are often required to make up unfinished work in class in addition to doing their nightly homework. Homework for children with ADHD is often a long, bitter, and unhappy task. As children advance in grades, homework battles become even more intense.

Affected children don't always understand directions or concepts given in the classroom, so they may spend an unwarranted amount of time calling classmates, looking for misplaced assignment sheets, or praying their parents are too busy or distracted to ask about the homework. Often, when parents do ask about homework, it can turn into World War III. The school counselor needs to recognize that addressing academic concerns in school often includes helping the child and parents find a way to "keep the peace" at home in regard to the child's homework.

Writing Challenges

Very often the first area of academic weakness that is identified in children with ADHD is written language (Lougy, DeRuvo, & Rosenthal, 2007). Because of the multiple skills involved in the writing process, it is an extremely taxing process. In addition, almost all academic areas require students to prove their knowledge in content matter through written response. Students who have weak writing skills rarely do well in their classes, even when they have strong content knowledge. These students struggle because of the need for strong executive-functioning skills (see Chapter 2) that help organize thoughts in a sequential manner. They often struggle to initiate written tasks because of EF difficulties in planning and defining the first step. To plan to write requires the need to evaluate and rephrase or paraphrase the assigned topic, think flexibly, and craft a complete thought that is "accessible to the 'absent audience'" (Meltzer & Krishnan, 2007). They also need the ability to capture those thoughts on paper before they fleetingly disappear. Students with ADHD are challenged by all these tasks because of delays in EF. Consequently, students with ADHD are rarely successful in this area without scaffolding and specific support (Lougy, DeRuvo, & Rosenthal, 2007).

In addition to struggling with the linguistic structure of writing, students who are required to write using a paper and pencil or pen may be limited only by their weaknesses in the area of fine motor skills. The skill required to form letters in writing is delayed and, in many cases, does not fully develop for these children (Lougy, DeRuvo, & Rosenthal, 2007; Lougy & Rosenthal, 2002). These students routinely have very sloppy penmanship; however, this is not because of laziness or a lack of caring but rather because of fine motor skills that are not fully developed. Dr. Mel Levine (2002), expert on children with learning differences, writes the following:

> Most obviously, some of the most complex muscular manipulations are demanded for writing. As we shall see, there are countless students with good ideas whose fingers just can't keep pace with their thinking, as a result of which they come to despise and avoid writing. (p. 171)

You also will find many upper-grade students with ADHD printing rather than using cursive writing. When these students are required to write in cursive, they often simply refuse to do assignments. These difficulties with fine motor skills lead to reluctant writers even if they have the concepts and ideas to write.

Experts agree that it is appropriate to circumvent students' difficulty with the physical act of writing by allowing students to dictate their compositions or write with a keyboard like an Alpha Smart (Fink-Chorzempa, Graham, & Harris, 2005). Bypassing writing and allowing the child to use other modalities and direct assistance from others is more beneficial than forcing a child with poor fine motor skills to spend an inordinate amount of time on writing.

Students with ADHD will find the organization necessary for writing difficult at all grade levels. Though creative, the process can seem overwhelming because of delays in sustained attention and intact executive functioning.

Strategies to Support Writing

1. Suggest that teachers use graphic organizers like those in Figure 4.1, sentence frames, framing questions, and word lists to support students in creating meaningful written work. Some students with ADHD will refuse to write or are unsuccessful with writing tasks when the teacher does not spend enough time on prewriting activities; using some of these strategies will make writing refusal less likely. It is essential that the teacher help the students develop content and a context for the writing topic before expecting the students to write.

   Providing scaffolding through specific structure and outline can be achieved through programs like Inspiration or Kidspiration (www.inspiration.com), which provide electronic scaffolding from brainstorming to outline format. These programs also provide visual support of pictures or icons as students create story webs and graphic organizers of their own. Other effective writing scaffolds and sentence and paragraph frames can be found at www.easyessay.com.

Figure 4.1

Venn Diagram Graphic Organizer

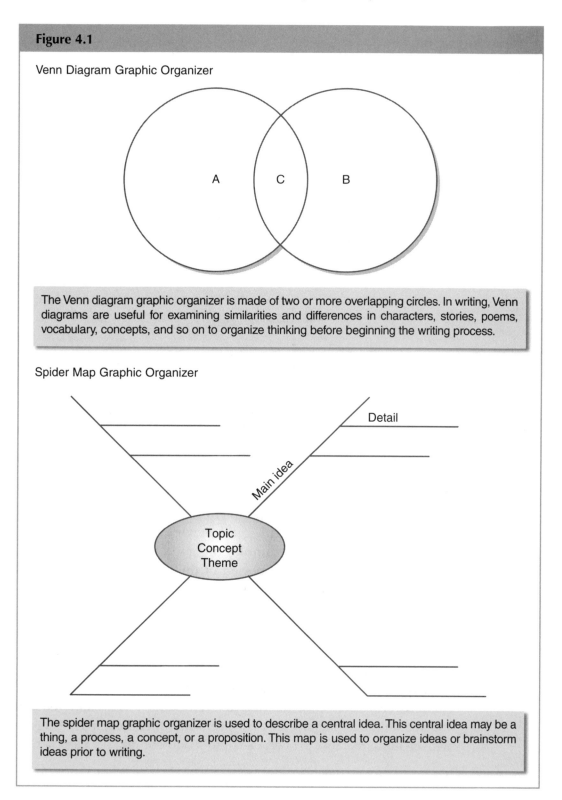

The Venn diagram graphic organizer is made of two or more overlapping circles. In writing, Venn diagrams are useful for examining similarities and differences in characters, stories, poems, vocabulary, concepts, and so on to organize thinking before beginning the writing process.

Spider Map Graphic Organizer

The spider map graphic organizer is used to describe a central idea. This central idea may be a thing, a process, a concept, or a proposition. This map is used to organize ideas or brainstorm ideas prior to writing.

(Continuted)

Figure 4.1 (Continued)

Cluster Graphic Organizer

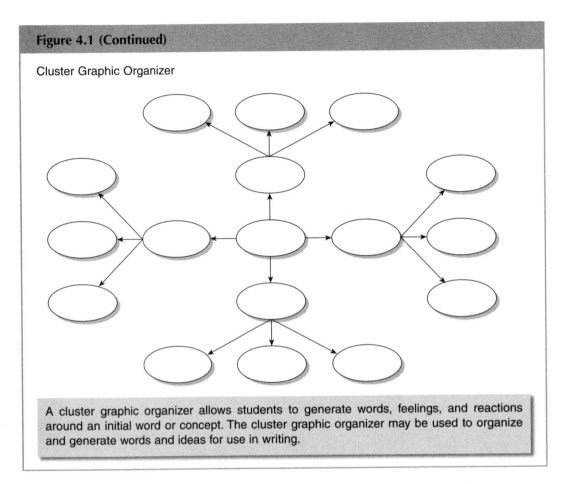

A cluster graphic organizer allows students to generate words, feelings, and reactions around an initial word or concept. The cluster graphic organizer may be used to organize and generate words and ideas for use in writing.

2. Suggest teachers provide a rubric with examples so students can see examples of good writing and poor writing and compare their writing to these exemplars. Even with good prewriting processes, students with ADHD need to see examples of "good writing" so that they can know exactly what is expected of them. Recommend that the teacher leave a finished model on the overhead or have models for students to look at available during the writing project.

3. Suggest that teachers provide an option for students to write expository, or if this is not an option, have the teacher provide scaffolds and models for support. Some students with ADHD will struggle with creative writing more than their peers. Many students with ADHD exhibit some developmental delays (Shaw, 2007). They may remain concrete thinkers longer than their peers and, therefore, may struggle with creating the abstract because of this slower brain development.

Reading Challenges

Although not as frequent as issues related to written language, reading comprehension, as a result of reading disabilities, is often cited as an area of weakness for students with ADHD (ldonline.org, 2008). In addition to the difficulty in understanding written words caused by the learning disability, comprehension also involves the need for sustained attention to the information being read. This task, which involves decoding and/or listening and holding information in short-term memory long enough to answer comprehension questions at the end of the chapter, can be a challenge!

As all of us find that our mind may wander when reading a passage, this happens with much more frequency and for a greater period of time for students who have ADHD. While we may go back and reread the passage to ensure we have obtained the salient information, students with ADHD may not find this gratifying enough to do and will just continue where they checked out, and later, they find that they are missing key pieces of information. These "holes" in the information affect their comprehension skills in reading and other content areas, creating a negative impact on their grades (Lougy, DeRuvo, & Rosenthal, 2007).

Strategies to Support Reading

1. Suggest that teachers use the audio text version of the textbook instead of silent reading of the text alone. Allowing the student to hear and read the information has a greater impact on memory and allows for improved attention.

2. Encourage teachers to always use some sort of graphic organizers while students read. This helps hold their attention, breaks the reading into digestible parts, and models for students how to identify the key literary constructs of setting, character, conflict, climax, and resolution. The visual support aids their recall of the story, the main idea and the sequence of events, when they are later required to summarize the story.

3. Suggest that teachers allow students to highlight the text while reading. This process helps the student to better attend to the text and helps them to find the important points when they are required to answer questions or fill in study guides. Many publishers provide the text in portable document format (pdf), so teachers would only need to print out these sections so that the students would not highlight in the textbook itself.

4. Suggest that teachers allow some students to use removable sticky dots or sticky notes to identify key points, main ideas, or new vocabulary during reading so that they can refer back to them later as needed (Rutherford, 2002).

Discuss with teachers the importance of stopping frequently while reading to review, summarize, and discuss. This will help students grasp key information to enhance comprehension, especially in content areas.

Math Challenges

Many students with ADHD struggle with math. In children with ADHD, 26% have a specific math disability (Mayes & Calhoun, 2006). In addition to often struggling with number sense, some of these children have difficulty mastering the basic addition, subtraction, multiplication, and division facts. Their retrieval of these math facts for other uses is slower than other students' (Swanson & Beebe-Frankenberger, 2004). These children have weaknesses in their working memory, leading to difficulty with word problems. In addition to problems with working memory, attentional problems, like the inability to block out extraneous stimuli from working memory, make math even more difficult (Platt, 2006). Furthermore, poor executive functioning affects math proficiency. Because of EF weaknesses, ADHD-affected students struggle with identifying the specific process steps necessary to solve problems. This makes math success that is dependent on "showing the work" difficult. These students can sometimes have the right answer, but cannot provide the step-by-step process on paper that is often required. They struggle with the tedium of solving a repetitive series of problems and the organizational skills needed to guarantee that no errors in calculation occur while solving problems on a small space on a piece of paper.

Because of difficulties with spatial organization, lack of good penmanship, and the ability to line up problems properly, many of these children will fail in math. They may look unmotivated when facing the daunting task of solving 20 or more problems that involve tedious steps, an undue amount of neatness for accuracy, and the excruciatingly boring task of showing all work. These students with ADHD are likely to give up before they start, find that they do not have the sustained attention to finish, or take hours to complete homework. This type of daily frustration can quickly lead students to develop a negative attitude toward math and their ability to be mathematically competent.

Strategies to Support Math

1. Allow students more space to solve problems. Many students, like children with ADHD, who struggle with fine motor and organizational skills find it very difficult to fit all the required work in the space provided on the worksheet. The space is usually too small,

making it difficult to keep work aligned properly. Suggest that teachers allow the students to use graph paper or dry erase boards to show their work, which provide the space and organization that they need to successfully set up and solve problems.

2. Allow students to solve fewer problems. Students with attention issues often work very slowly. It may take them three hours to finish the same amount of work that other students can do in 30 minutes. Suggest that teachers reduce the number of problems to be fair when considering the time it takes to complete the same number of problems.

3. Allow students to show work on only a few problems. Students with ADHD may solve things differently. They often can see the answer or can solve it in their heads but struggle with explaining the step-by-step process that they have used. Requiring them to show their work for all problems becomes a very time-consuming task. Suggest that the teacher allow them to solve one problem using the show-their-work process and then allow them to write just the answers for the rest.

4. Provide students worksheets with problems already written. Some students with ADHD struggle significantly with copying problems accurately from the textbook to the binder paper. If they copy the problem wrong, they have no chance of getting the answer correct. Suggesting that the teacher provide a photocopy or adapted worksheet with the problems on it would avoid this problem.

Check for Understanding

All students, including students with ADHD, need ample modeling and frequent checks for understanding during the instruction process. This process holds the children's attention and can be easily accomplished through the use of student whiteboards. Suggest that teachers use this process to ensure that students are clear on what is expected of them before they begin the independent practice.

RELATED ACADEMIC PERFORMANCE AREAS CHALLENGING FOR CHILDREN WITH ADHD

Children with ADHD are often challenged by schools tasks that require self-monitoring, time management, organization, and sustained and focused attention. These areas alone can keep some students from being academically successful. Some of these areas that seem most problematic are discussed as well as some practical strategies that students can develop that will help them overcome these challenges.

Independent Studying, Homework, and Long-Term Projects

All these tasks are dependent on EF processes and require the student to plan ahead, predict outcomes, and set long-term goals. Independent projects can be especially challenging because they include a number of EFs: organization, time management, having the material to do the project, completing the task on time, and remembering to turn it in for credit (Meltzer, 2007). The counselor can support students by helping them break down tasks into doable parts by developing a calendar of deadlines based on small chunks of the project or assignment.

Because of difficulty with time management, few ADHD-affected students have any idea how long a task will take (both short- and long-term assignments). Most often, they will misjudge or exaggerate the amount of time they will need (Garber, Garber, & Spizman, 1996). Helping an affected student gauge how long a project will take will alleviate a lot of fear and frustration around homework and projects. One recommendation is to have students look over their assignments and estimate how long they think it will take them to complete. They write the minutes on the back of the assignment sheet. When they begin the task, they write down the starting time on the left corner of the first page, and when it is completed, they jot down the ending time. This will help students learn to estimate time for completing projects and also will help them with sustained and focused attention. The counselor can coach the student and parents on this process, and with time, a student normally finds more success in judging time for completing school assignments.

Test Taking

Successful test taking requires a number of EFs that are often delayed in affected children: staying alert and engaged, time management, identifying the most important information to study, self-monitoring, and completing the test efficiently (Meltzer, 2007). The accommodations of extra time and the opportunity to take tests in parts are appropriate to recommend for students with ADHD.

RECOGNIZING LEARNING STYLES

In addition to specific strategies related to particular content areas, teachers will find that more students learn when they recognize different learning styles and provide differentiated instruction (see Chapter 3) that meets the needs of all types of learners. Most teachers teach in their modality-strength style. Those teachers who are auditory learners will do a lot of lecture; those who are more visual learners will use a lot of visual tools, like the overhead projector; and kinesthetic-type teachers are usually the most fun because they like to involve movement in their teaching. Traditionally, it has been the auditory, language-centered learner who usually ended up choosing teaching as a career, and our classrooms are filled with teachers who rely heavily on language and listening to obtain content knowledge.

As we come to recognize different types of learners from the early research on multiple intelligences by Howard Gardner (1993) and Rita Dunn and Kenneth Dunn's research (1978) on learning styles, we can easily see that being able to identify learning styles and using them as a basis for instruction is vitally important for teachers in light of an increasingly diverse student population.

We will only briefly cover the three primary learning styles, researched by Dunn and Dunn (1978), and provide you with information that you can easily share with a teacher who has brought a student to the problem-solving team.

The following examples provide help for both the students and their teacher in helping them identify and use their learning preferences successfully in instructional planning and learning.

Visual Learners

- Prefer sitting at the front of the classroom to avoid visual obstructions (e.g., people's heads)
- Think in pictures and learn best from visual displays like graphic organizers
- Need the use of visual materials, such as pictures, charts, maps, graphs, diagrams, flow charts, PowerPoint, video clips, flipcharts, and handouts
- Should have a clear view of the teacher's body language and facial expression when he or she is speaking
- Use color to highlight important points in text
- Prefer to take notes or have the teacher provide handouts to absorb information

- Illustrate ideas as a picture or brainstorming bubble before writing them down
- Write stories and illustrate them
- Use multimedia (e.g., computers, videos, TeacherTube, and YouTube)
- Study in a quiet place away from verbal disturbances
- Read illustrated books
- Visualize information as pictures to aid memorization

Auditory Learners

- Think logically, analytically, and sequentially
- Participate in class discussions/debates
- Are task oriented
- Make speeches and presentations
- Use tape recorders during lectures instead of taking notes
- Read text out aloud
- Create musical jingles and/or mnemonics to aid memorization
- Discuss ideas verbally
- Dictate to someone while they write down their thoughts
- Use verbal analogies and storytelling to demonstrate a point

Tactile/Kinesthetic Learners

- Think globally
- Take frequent study breaks
- Move around to learn new things (e.g., read while on an exercise bike, mold a piece of clay to learn a new concept)
- Work in a standing position
- Chew gum while studying
- Use bright colors to highlight reading material
- Dress up their work space with posters
- Listen to music while studying
- Skim through reading material to get a rough idea what it is about before settling down to read it in detail
- Struggle with logical, analytical, and sequential tasks until they see the big picture
- Make creative and unusual associations with the subject at hand

Once teachers begin to realize that classrooms are filled with these diverse learners, it is easier to bring about the concept of adjusting instruction to meet the needs of students who learn in a variety of ways. It may also help them to see that some behaviors that they may have associated with willful disobedience may actually be a manifestation of the child's learning style. For example, children who are always drawing may be seen as not paying attention or being distracted, but when children are drawing pictures that help them absorb the content, or children who respond with off-the-wall responses, they may be incorporating the global learning style of tactile kinesthetic learners.

So what suggestions can you, the school counselor, make to teachers who are now aware of the diversity in their classroom and are willing to change the way they teach? Next you will find suggestions for multimodality instruction to support the increased success of students with ADHD and others who struggle with auditory instruction alone.

MULTIMODALITY TEACHING STRATEGIES

It is important to impress on teachers that they should consider using multimodality instruction in every lesson they teach. If the teacher spends most of the class time lecturing and discussing orally, the most frequently used mode of instruction, only those with linguistic learning strengths benefit. When asked to consult, you can make the following suggestions to the classroom teacher for the students you are working with.

1. Incorporate visuals in every lesson. Recommend that the teacher talk for only 10–15 minutes, then support the instruction through the use of visuals, such as a video or other multimedia for another block of time. Using PowerPoint, interactive blackboards, and other digital media supports the needs of visual learners. Visual support for content is easily obtained by downloading images from Google images, and numerous Web sites offer free or minimally priced video clips for classroom use. YouTube, iTunes, and TeacherTube also have some options for video images for instructional purposes (http://www.teachertube.com).

2. Provide appropriate background music while kids are working. For many students, memory and learning are enhanced when certain types of music play softly in the background. Particularly effective are classical and jazz music, but any kind of relaxing music is effective. If music is a distraction to the auditory learners, recommend they wear headphones or have them listen to environmental sounds or white noise.

3. Provide hands-on experience as often as possible. Recommend teachers investigate ways that students can interact with the content in some concrete and active way. Students can build models, play games that require movement, or act out a particular concept. Simple movement can take a boring, mundane task to one that is engaging and inviting. One example might include taking the answers for a study guide and posting them in different places around the classroom. Having students move in groups to find the answers to their scavenger hunt study guide will still provide the content instruction but now involves movement and group cooperation. Incorporating physical movement activities in the classroom helps all students, including those with ADHD, to be better focused and to stay on task for longer periods of time (Mulrine, Prater, & Jenkins, 2008).

4. Encourage teachers to have students share how they have solved a problem or explain how they arrived at an answer. Students learn from teaching/explaining to others what they have learned. Sharing with at least one partner ensures that the concept is truly understood and supports transfer to long-term memory. If students can teach someone else, the teacher can be sure that they have worked through the thinking process and have mastered the concepts. Teachers need to be aware that a productive, engaged classroom may be a noisy one!

5. Offer a good balance between cooperative learning and independent work. Some students, especially those with ADHD, find that the opportunity to work with others helps them overcome some of the barriers that they often face. The frequent interaction with others, the opportunity to verbally share, and the chance to move are ideal learning situations for many students who do not work best independently.

6. Give students time, regularly, to reflect on what has been taught and learned. Having students reflect on their learning is another good strategy that supports integrating new concepts to memory. It is important for teachers to remember that while some students will choose to record their reflections in a journal, others would prefer to create a sketch or model or just verbally share with a partner. Insisting that students write in journals many times each week favors linguistic and visual learners but discriminates against artistic and kinesthetic students.

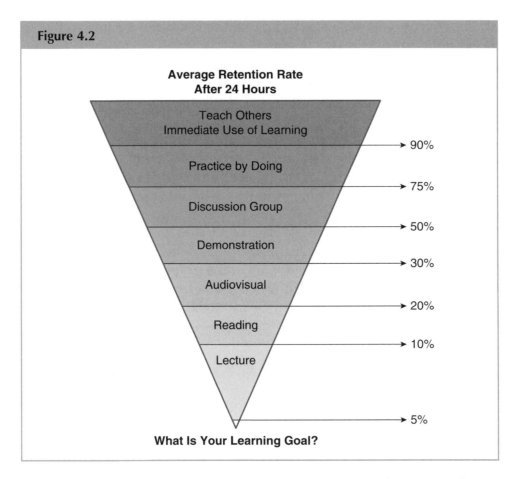

Figure 4.2

Average Retention Rate After 24 Hours

Teach Others
Immediate Use of Learning → 90%

Practice by Doing → 75%

Discussion Group → 50%

Demonstration → 30%

Audiovisual → 20%

Reading → 10%

Lecture → 5%

What Is Your Learning Goal?

Considering the average retention rate of content information after 24 hours based on using multimodal teaching strategies (see Figure 4.2), the counselor advocating for a young client with ADHD would be wise to recommend that teachers employ these strategies. Teachers will realize that students learn more, retain more, and become content competent more quickly when they employ these strategies that meet the learning styles of all students in the classroom, especially the learning styles of their students with ADHD.

TIME MANAGEMENT AND ORGANIZATIONAL SKILLS

Although students with ADHD have the ability to learn the core content in their classrooms, the report cards often do not reflect this fact. If counselors delve a bit further into the reasons for failing grades, they will find it is often a result of missing assignments rather than poor performance on classroom work or tests. It is the lack of organizational skills that causes students with ADHD to fail classes rather than laziness or lack of ability.

But how can the counselor impact the skills needed for the student to improve their organization? In some cases, it takes teaching the teacher and other students how to support affected students in helping them to remember when to turn things in and how to write and keep track of assignments. In some cases, it takes direct instruction on organizational practices, and in many cases, it takes ongoing monitoring until the students develop organizational habits of their own.

There are many expert resources available on developing organizational skills. Patty Schetter (2004), in her work with students diagnosed with high functioning autism, has developed a number of graphic organizers that help students break tasks down into doable parts (see Figures 4.3 and 4.4). This process has been found to be very effective for students with ADHD who struggle with the development of executive functioning skills. The visual support of the graphic organizer can take the overwhelming and muddled concept of writing a report to an organized structured activity that can be managed despite the many steps involved (Schetter, 2004).

Figure 4.3

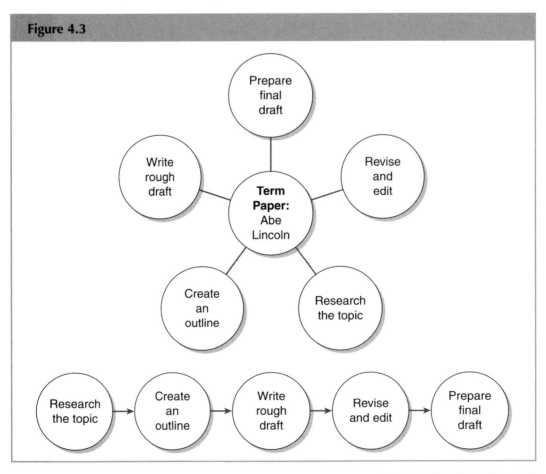

Reprinted with permission, Patricia Schetter, MA, Autism Behavior Training Associates

Figure 4.4

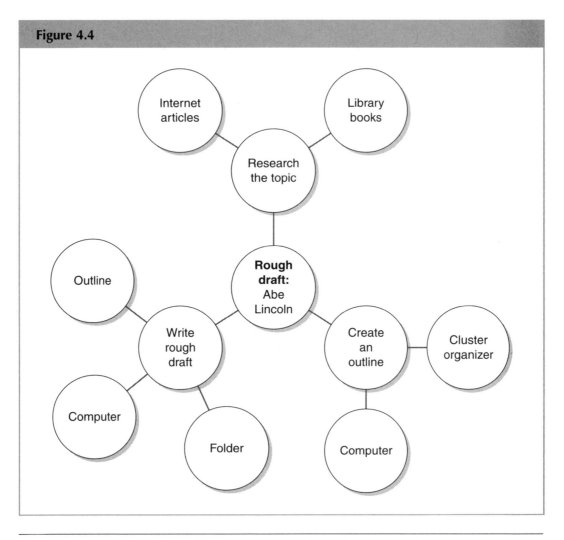

Reprinted with permission, Patricia Schetter, MA, Autism Behavior Training Associates

In addition to using graphic organizers and the time-estimation-scheduling strategies developed by Patty Schetter (2004) (see Figure 4.5), students can also help develop their own organizational skills through practice and training in the use of these specific strategies.

It may take trying several different types of organizational strategies and tools until the student can identify one that will work for them. Ease of use seems to be of utmost importance when trying to develop organizational skills for students with ADHD. If the organizational structure takes extra time or extra steps, it will probably not be used effectively. For some time, many schools were attempting to enforce binder organizational skills for all students. Although teachers and parents may find that binders and binder dividers are their best form of organization, students often do not want to take the extra time to punch holes in all papers and file them in the correct folder or tab, and subsequently, papers disappeared into the black hole of the backpack. Students with ADHD may do better with getting papers into colored Velcro folders rather than binders. When the Velcro folders are color coded with textbook covers, students have a better chance of getting the correct books and papers home and back to school. Some students will also need a specific color folder for papers that need to be turned in.

Figure 4.5

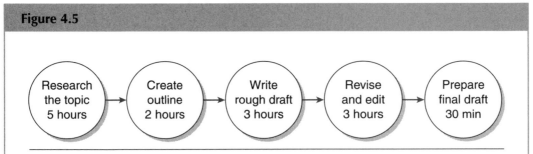

Reprinted with permission, Patricia Schetter, MA, Autism Behavior Training Associates

September 2009						
Sunday	**Monday**	**Tuesday**	**Wednesday**	**Thursday**	**Friday**	**Saturday**
		1	2	3	4	5
		Research Lincoln (3:00–5:00)	**Research Lincoln (3:00–4:00)** Soccer practice (5:00–6:00)	Study spelling	Spelling test Free time (4:00–6:00)	Soccer game (12:00–1:00) Beach trip (cancelled)
6	7	8	9	10	11	12
Research Lincoln (3:00–5:00) Beach trip (cancelled)	**Write outline to Lincoln report (4:00–6:00)**	**Outline for Lincoln report due**	Study calculus Soccer practice (5:00–6:00)	Study spelling Study calculus	Spelling test Free time (4:00–6:00)	Soccer game (8:00–9:00) Beach trip (11:00)
13	14	15	16	17	18	19
Beach trip Study calculus	Calculus test **Work on Lincoln rough draft (5:00–6:00)**	**Work on Lincoln rough draft (4:00–5:00)**	Study spelling Soccer practice (5:00–6:00)	**Rough draft for Lincoln report due** Study spelling	Spelling test Free time (4:00–6:00)	Soccer game (9:00–10:00) Soccer picnic (1:00–4:00)

Sunday	Monday	Tuesday	Wednesday	Thursday	Friday	Saturday
20	21	22	23	24	25	26
Work on book report (9:00–12:00) Movies (2:00–5:00)	Work on book report (4:00–6:00)	Work on book report (4:00–6:00)	Study spelling Soccer practice (5:00–6:00)	Book report due Study spelling	Spelling test Free time (4:00–6:00)	Soccer game (10:00–11:00)
27	28	29	30			
Revisions to Lincoln report (9:00–12:00)	Dr. Appt. (3:30) **Prepare final Lincoln report (5:30–6:00)**	**Final draft for Lincoln report due**	Study spelling Soccer practice (5:00–6:00)			

Plot out the steps (including due dates and work time) on the monthly calendar. Boldface indicates components of the Abe Lincoln report; all other information consists of regularly and irregularly occurring events and other complex assignments that were previously scheduled.

Despite all attempts to organize with the multitude of folders and organizers available today, some students find that keeping the papers in the textbook is the most foolproof way to ensure that papers and books get home together and that papers get turned in when the textbook is taken out for class the next day. Although the paper edges may be a bit crunched, there is a higher likelihood that papers get home, get back to school, and get turned in utilizing this tried-and-true strategy. It takes flexibility on the part of the adults to accept papers that have wrinkled edges, but this is a small price to pay for helping a student find a successful way to complete assignments and get them turned in.

SUMMARY

As the school counselor, you will play an integral role in helping your young clients with ADHD be successful in the classroom. In the consultative role that you play at your school site, you can serve as an effective, helpful resource to teachers and parents who desire to find ways to improve the daily classroom experience and, ultimately, the outcomes for their students. Providing insightful information on the learning needs of these students will provide teachers with the tools they need to change their instruction to meet the specific learning needs of their students with ADHD. With knowledge, information, and instructional strategies geared toward diverse learners, the classroom can become a productive, enjoyable, and successful place for learning to occur, making failing grades and poor classroom performance a thing of the past for your young clients with ADHD.

5 Managing ADHD Behaviors in the School Setting

It's *impossible* to fully understand the behavior of children with ADHD without giving careful consideration to their disorder. For one thing, it exemplifies a very real challenge where they find themselves caught between two polarities: One involves becoming aware of their disorder and how it affects and makes everyday chores and activities more challenging, and the other is being expected by adults to try their best and "make no excuses," often receiving little support, empathy, or understanding from teachers and other adults in their life. This dilemma will often torment affected children. Sometimes, they can find some resolution at an intellectual level, but at their innermost emotional being, it can leave deep scars. Consequently, it's critically important to recognize that any classroom or schoolwide BIP needs to temper affected students' disruptive and sometimes dangerous behaviors but not be so Draconian as to damage their self-esteem and emotional well-being. We hope the interventions provided in this chapter will allow you, as you advocate for children with ADHD, to meet this important goal.

It's also important to recognize that while working with affected children, they will bring to your counseling room feelings of rejection and victimization stemming back many years. They may say, "I don't know," when asked about a misdeed, but this is often only a defense mechanism stemming from feelings of fear, rejection, and anxiety. Some children will be frozen in silence or will truly be unsure of what they have done wrong or may be unable to truly identify their emotions. The counselor needs to be patient, willing to wait for these children to feel comfortable and safe before they can even begin to verbalize what they fear. They may be full of anger, hostility, and frustration and may express themselves in a manner that seems inappropriate. Punishing them for these "bad thoughts" will only stop any further opportunities for resolution and problem solving, so this type of behavior will need to be handled with much care and finesse. It is important to help them recognize that you are a *safe* person to talk to but also that you require respect and consideration.

Whether or not they speak, many ADHD-affected children have minds that are spinning fast forward and out of control. Not speaking is one way they will communicate that they are worried about what is happening. Some of their ideas will be realistic, some misplaced or exaggerated, and some will be so full of anger that they cannot even identify them. Keep in mind that there are no empty spaces in their minds. Even when they say, "I don't know," they can have ideas that are too scary or unacceptable to articulate. They may happily lie to you about what they feel if they think it will bring immediate comfort and relief from prodding questions.

Let's Begin

School counselors are often initially asked to work with children with ADHD because of their disruptive behaviors. Children with ADHD often find themselves in trouble at school for any number of reasons, some incidents more serious than others.

Ryan, Second Grade

Ryan, an eight-year-old second grader, was reprimanded by his teacher for *again* not remembering to come in at recess when the bell rang. A classmate had to run out to the playground equipment and let him know that Ms. Brown, his teacher, was waiting for him to line up.

Brian, Seventh Grade

Brian was *again* sent to the office for yelling out at his teacher when upset. He had a long history of problematic behaviors—oppositional attitude toward teachers, fights on the playground, and showing "lack of motivation to change."

Carol, Tenth Grade

Carol's teachers were *always* asking Carol to listen and not interrupt or disrupt her classmates from learning. Even after repeated warnings, nothing seemed to work for long. Her teachers described Carol as a "good kid," but "always needing reminders to be quiet and get back to work."

Teachers of children with ADHD often present ongoing concerns around compliance, anger control, disruptive behaviors, negative peer interactions, and, for some affected children, lying, stealing, and destroying school property. Often schools have no answers for dealing with these behaviors other than punishment. These children often find themselves suspended, expelled, and the recipients of any number of other interventions by teachers, administrators, and parents trying to address their negative and disruptive behaviors. Generally, these behaviors are more annoying than dangerous, but even the most innocuous behaviors will test a teacher's patience after repeated offenses. Some examples of ADHD behavioral and academic traits are listed in Table 5.1, Behavioral and Academic Profile of ADHD Children—Grades K–12.

Even though there are numerous behavioral areas that can be addressed, the ones shared in this chapter are the most problematic and often require the counselor's attention in a school setting.

POSITIVE SCHOOLWIDE INTERVENTION

Schoolwide positive behavior supports (SWPBS) (Sugai et al., 2000) provide a comprehensive systematic positive behavior plan across a school setting. These schoolwide positive supports are based on clear and consistent behavioral expectations that all adults have of all children. This type of systematic support can go far to help all children in and out of the classroom develop appropriate social behaviors. Clear behavioral expectations are supported by evidence-based, high-quality instructional practices that help students learn through active engagement.

Some students with ADHD will still struggle with maintaining and controlling behaviors even with schoolwide positive behavior supports. For these students, a secondary level of intervention should be made available before moving toward more intensive tertiary interventions. These secondary interventions usually require minimal time to implement, incorporate similar features across various student groups, and provide extra doses of positive supports (Fairbanks, Simonsen, & Sugai, 2008). These strategies usually include an increase in daily structure, provision of more frequent behavioral prompts, and frequent doses of praise for appropriate behaviors.

Table 5.1   Behavioral and Academic Profile of ADHD Children—Grades K–12

Behavioral

- Have difficulty waiting their turn
- Interrupt or intrude on others (violates space or boundaries) (*DSM-IV-TR,* 2000)
- Cannot wait for the teacher to call their name or pay attention to them
- Need constant reinforcement and have difficulty with delayed gratification
- Make errors on assignments in an effort to finish quickly
- Have difficulty tempering unhappy feelings (e.g., inappropriate language, yelling, throwing things)
- Rush through one thing to another in play
- Cannot sustain attention and have trouble listening
- Show better attention on novel, interesting tasks or during one-on-one activities
- Have difficulty maintaining effort aligned with difficulty maintaining concentration
- Have "an attentional bias toward novelty" (Robin, 1998, pp. 17–18)
- Cannot delay gratification—driven by the moment: "ready, aim, fire kids (Lavoie, 2005)
- Are easily distracted
- Often act as if "driven by a motor" or are "often on the go" (*DSM-IV-TR,* 2000)
- Demonstrate excessive activity levels
- Inadvertently break things
- Constantly fidget
- May show impaired coordination
- Can have poor eye-hand coordination
- Blurt out in class or interrupt
- Have difficulty regulating their behavior in accordance with external/internal rules
- Are easily frustrated
- Tend to be reckless and prone to accidents—act before thinking
- Fail to comply, usually because of forgetfulness or distraction
- Respond to immediate reinforcement but effects are temporary
- Can have a cycle of negative interactions between caretakers
- Sometimes seen as bossy, stubborn, selfish, bullying, and annoying
- Show social immaturity—often acting two to three years younger than his or her their chronological age (Barkley, 1995)
- Have difficulty making and keeping friends—can become socially isolated and can be seen playing alone at recess or lunch
- Show great need for attention and sometimes act as the class clown
- Lack awareness of others' feelings, behaviors, or motivations
- Have labile moods—emotionally overactive, lose temper, accompanied by aggressive or violent outbursts (not like episodic moods swings seen in bipolar individuals)
- May become overexcited and lose control when happy

- Hum, whistle, or make other noises in class
- Daydream or get lost in their thoughts, are sluggish, and stare blankly (behaviors observed generally in children with ADHD-I)
- Tend to be nervous, high strung, and tense
- Often play with younger children

Academic

- Lose or forget to write down assignments
- Blurt out answers before questions have been given
- Do not finish work on time
- Do not organize assignments well
- Have trouble keeping paperwork and records complete
- Have messy desks and/or backpacks
- Show less attention to boring tasks and routine classwork than unaffected classmates because of developmental delays in focused and sustained attention
- Can have poor handwriting
- Rush through assignments overlooking crucial details and make careless mistakes
- Take longer time doing homework
- Tend to be late finishing or turning in work assignments
- Can become overwhelmed deciding what to do first—leading to unfinished work
- Have difficulty recalling learned material
- Have difficulty transitioning from one subject area to another
- May be seen as apathetic or unmotivated by teachers and parents
- Have poor test-taking skills because of chronic difficulties with selective, focused, and sustained attention
- Do not work up to potential, underachievers
- Fail to carry out assigned tasks/chores
- Have difficulty following teacher's directions
- May be challenged by written language tasks, reading and math problems, spelling, and reading comprehension
- Have difficulty with time management and organization
- Have difficulty copying from the whiteboard and listening at the same time
- Opt for short-term pleasure despite long-term pain
- May not relate positively to teachers or authority figures
- Do not bring necessary materials to class
- Have difficulty completing long-term assignments
- Tend to be late to class (especially middle and high school)
- Do not cooperate or participate in class because of elevated oppositional behaviors, high distractibility, or low motivation to schoolwork
- Show resistance to accepting assistance (especially in middle and high school)
- Have difficulty asking questions or communicating their needs

Check In, Check Out (CICO)

A common example of a secondary intervention is Check In, Check Out (CICO), also known as the behavior education program (BEP) (Hawken & Horner, 2003). It is a schoolwide intervention that all staff members are aware of and that potentially any student, including those with ADHD, can utilize. The intervention is targeted at students who engage in relatively low-level disruptive problem behaviors, such as blurting out, irregular work completion, tardiness, and off-task behaviors, which are frequent problem areas for students with ADHD.

The CICO procedure involves students *checking in* with an adult at the beginning of each school day. During this time, expectations are reviewed, daily goals for behavior are developed, and the adult ensures the students have the materials they need for the day. At regular time intervals throughout the day, the students are given points and specific performance feedback. At the end of the day, the students *check out* with this same adult by reviewing the point sheet, determining if the goals were met, providing acknowledgment, and providing a copy of the card to go home to parents (Fairbanks, Simonsen, & Sugai, 2008).

The data from these daily charts are compiled so that weekly the students are able to analyze their own behavior, recognize their strengths and weaknesses, and try to identify patterns that cause their behavioral difficulties. This ongoing monitoring and data analysis helps the students develop self-management skills and take a greater responsibility for their own behavior. Over time, the behavior moves from a teacher- or counselor-managed system to a student-managed system.

Students with ADHD benefit greatly from this type of secondary intervention. With adequate support from teachers and the school counselor, many students will not need further or more specific interventions. The initial or primary schoolwide positive behavior approach can be the first step to improving behavioral outcomes for all students. More information on this process can be found at www.pbis.org. Secondary interventions are needed for approximately 11% of elementary students, 26% of middle school students, and 29% of high school students (Horner, 2007). Students with ADHD often fall into the 5% to 10% of the student population that require more intensive tertiary interventions, which are more student specific and require the intervention of professionals like the school counselor. The following interventions are intended to meet the more intensive needs of this student population.

POSITIVE INDIVIDUAL INTERVENTIONS

Students with ADHD often need more individualized interventions to address problem-based behaviors. Here are recommended interventions that address a range of ADHD behaviors commonly brought to the school counselor's attention.

Difficulty With Anger Management

Many children with ADHD have a difficult time controlling their emotions. Their emotions tend to be extreme and poorly filtered. They seem to ride an emotional roller coaster, riding up and down like a yo-yo, causing those around them to walk on eggshells for fear something or someone will set them off.

> *Ryan, a 13-year-old seventh grader, recalls telling his counselor that he doesn't understand why he can't stop himself from yelling at his teacher or his classmate when upset. He feels upset afterword and knows that "the other kids probably think he is a jerk." He states, "I have spent all my life having people angry with me because I can't stop saying or doing mean things when I am angry."*
>
> *His teachers sometimes were fooled by Ryan's swagger and found themselves dismissing his apologies—seeing it as just his way of trying to stay out of trouble. Ryan, after many episodes, expressed to his counselor that he found himself clamming up more and more and refusing to say anything, except, "Call my parents, I don't care." His inner pain and embarrassment were masked by body language and words that portrayed a child who didn't care about his behaviors and who had no desire to change.*

Children, like Ryan, have difficulty expressing their emotions verbally, so unhappy feelings build up and *sometimes* present themselves in violent outbursts or expressions of cursing, teasing, and name-calling, often sending other students running to the teacher for support. The punishment and disapproval for these kinds of outbursts, unfortunately, usually only escalate the problems and often lead to more elevated outbursts and behavior (Lougy & Rosenthal, 2002).

As a school counselor, you will be asked to help these students find ways to temper or better control their anger. Helping students temper angry feelings and outbursts is not always easy or problem free. Affected students, even when on medication, often will have more difficulty controlling their anger, compared to unaffected classmates, because of their ADHD.

Responsibilities of Adults

A team approach is required for an intervention to be successful and effective. This team needs to include the student, teacher, parents, counselor, and doctor (if the child is on medication). An intervention that only includes the student, no matter what age or grade level, will often fall short of meeting its goal—developing behaviors that help the student stop or minimize disruptive and/or angry outburst at school.

Responsibilities of Students

The degree and level of involvement by the students depend on the maturity and age of the students. Early latency-age children often do not have the maturity to self-regulate or monitor their outbursts; whereas children over the age of 9 or 10 can begin to take a more active role in their treatment. Children 12 years old, for example, are going to benefit from learning tools to deal with their anger better than children six years old.

The counselor can play a pivotal role helping students with ADHD deal with name-calling, saying "no" to stay out of trouble, learning self-control activities (self-directed talk), and learning to self-identify emotions when they are getting upset. These tasks, however, require the school counselor to understand the primary handicapping conditions contributing to the children's difficulties around anger management and self-control. It goes without saying that the counselor has to have developed a positive trust relationship with the students before any intervention can be successful. This process may take some time, but it is integral to any positive behavior change process. Some students are very defensive when talking about their problems and find it very difficult to open up. Counselors should not become angry and frustrated with students who are silent, as even silence is a form of communication. Over time, most affected students will learn to trust the counselor and will find that the counselor can provide a safe and respectful environment where they can candidly share their most pressing problems.

Importance of the Children Understanding Their Diagnosis

An important first step in helping affected children deal with their emotions and learning challenges is to take time to talk with the children about their diagnosis. A counselor will discover that some children are very knowledgeable about their diagnosis, while other children will have limited understanding. Some children will also be in denial. Children who are in denial are often resistant to interventions and school support. It's important that they begin to discuss their feelings around this area so that they are more open to school interventions to help them.

The authors have found the following suggestions helpful when talking with children about their diagnosis.

- Let children know that they are not the only child diagnosed with ADHD at school and you are helping other children who are diagnosed with ADHD at school.

- Be prepared to discuss both the children's strengths as well as their challenges stemming from their disorder. However, remember that ADHD reflects only part of children's performance and personality. There are many factors that can explain and contribute to poor school performance and behavior.

- It's helpful to have a copy of the *DSM-IV-TR* (2000) criteria for diagnosing ADHD. The authors have found that when students see in writing some of those traits that describe their behaviors, it can help them move beyond denial and to acceptance. However, like any intervention, it's important that the counselor has established a caring and supportive relationship with the children before trying this suggestion.

- Remember that the age of the children should determine the amount of information shared with them. Like suggested earlier for parents, children under the age of nine years often only need a general reference to their disorder. (e.g., "Bobby, your mother shared you are diagnosed with ADHD. Children with ADHD sometimes find it difficult to keep their feelings in check. Let's see if we can work on ways for you not to get so angry at recess when upset.") With older children, you can be more specific when discussing how their disorder can affect learning and behavior. (e.g., "Sarah, children with ADHD will sometimes need additional time for test taking. Sarah, like other students with ADHD, you sometimes will become distracted in class and not be able to finish your test. This is why Ms. Reynolds is letting you go to the library to finish your history test when not completed.")

- Occasionally counselors will encounter teenagers who refuse to take their ADHD medication despite observations by school staff and parents who note dramatic improvement in ADHD symptoms while the teenagers are on the medication. In many of these cases, there doesn't seem to be any apparent side effects from the medication (such as loss of appetite or headaches) and the dose seems to have been adjusted properly for optimal improvement in attention and focus. They will say, "It's not doing anything," "It doesn't make any difference," "I just don't feel like myself on the medication," or "I am not funny anymore." Further questioning may reveal that the underlying issue, particularly in hyperactive and impulsive teenagers, is that the improvement in impulse control is being interpreted by the adolescent as a "loss of spontaneity" when interacting with peers (i.e., children are no longer acting like the class clown). For teenagers who are uncomfortable with this change, sometimes the best initial compromise is to lower the medication dosage slightly so that the teens can still feel like they have maintained their spontaneity while still benefiting from improvement in ADHD symptoms from the medication.

In conclusion, it's important that you have more than one conversation with children about their diagnosis. Often circumstances will provide an opening to talk with children about how their disorder may have been a contributing factor in explaining their actions or decision. However, ADHD is not a "get-out-of-jail-free" card. Affected children need to know that they are responsible for their actions. The counselor can help students find better ways to problem solve, but the counselor should not make excuses for aggressive or noncompliant behaviors.

INTERVENTIONS CAN HELP WITH CONTROLLING ANGER

Primary Grades

The authors' experience is that for students up to the third grade, the primary agents for behavioral change are the counselor, teacher, and parents. For this reason, it is of utmost importance that all three parties work together. Caretakers need to understand that because of neurodevelopmental factors, younger children have not generally developed what is commonly referred to as an *internal locus of control*. Younger children often perceive consequences as the result of others and not as something they have any control over, and therefore, they often do not claim any responsibility for their own behaviors and actions. Over time, and through experience, children gain the understanding that they themselves can control outcomes, that is, they can influence what happens to them. External behavioral interventions and reinforcers (tokens, positive behavior monitoring sheets), social stories (Gray, 2006) (http://www.thegraycenter.org), and positive verbal and nonverbal reinforcement can be very helpful in addressing or minimizing problem-based behaviors in young children.

Young children are often not self-starters or self-stoppers and need the intervention and direct support of adults to help them learn how to regulate their behavior. A teacher should not expect young children to always do the right thing, even if they know what the right thing to do is. Young affected students will often know what to do—they just have great difficulty doing it consistently.

The authors have found that when placing interventions in a school setting, such as the classroom or playground area, it's best to keep them simple and consistent. When interventions are too detailed and require too much monitoring or time commitment by the teacher or other staff members, they often are not followed through with consistently—and they ultimately fail. Consequently, the interventions provided below are simple methods a counselor can share with a teacher that have been used successfully by the authors. They generally require little time management by the classroom teacher.

Green, Yellow, and Red Cards (Grades K–3)

Cut strips of green, yellow, and red paper in to 2×8 lengths. The paper should be available for the teacher or children to access when angry feelings are being observed or expected. The green strip indicates children's feelings are under control and they are in a happy state of mind. The yellow strip suggests they are not sure and may be close to losing their temper or are beginning to get upset and angry. The red strip means they are in an angry state of mind and need time by themselves to calm down. The children, if feeling angry, can pick a yellow or red strip, indicating to their teacher how they are feeling. They then can be given permission to leave the group activity and find a quiet spot (calm-down area) to be alone until they feel less angry or agitated. This technique can help children begin to better self-monitor their feelings and provide them an acceptable way to deal with their feelings. The teacher often is more directly involved with younger children (i.e., handing them a colored strip if the teacher observes the children getting agitated).

In this intervention, the students can also be encouraged to use catchy anger-controlling, self-talk statements after the students have evaluated each situation as green, yellow, or red. For example, Dr. Taylor (2006) recommends, in a similar intervention he developed (red light, yellow light, green light technique), that children be taught to say catchy self-talk words such as "zip my lips, turn around, and leave" for a red strip situation; "stay calm" and "stay in control" for yellow strip situation; and "go ahead and enjoy" for a green strip situation.

This intervention should be done intermittently throughout the school day. It can also be used to reinforce positive choices. Children are rewarded or praised by the teacher/parent for going to their calm-down area without getting upset or argumentative. The goal is to provide children positive ways to deal with angry feelings, not to punish.

Robot-Rag Doll Technique

This technique is best used with children nine years old and younger. It can be practiced individually or as a group (circle time). The robot-rag doll technique is a useful muscle tension/relaxation approach with young children. This technique can also be reinforced and practiced in the counselor's office or at home with the parents.

The teacher or counselor asks the children to tense all muscles in the body and visualize themselves as robots and to hold this tense state for approximately 15 seconds. Then the children are asked to release all the tension and visualize themselves as a rag doll with all their muscles very loose. The children should hold this relaxed state for 15 seconds. The teacher or counselor should allow time to practice this technique until the children seem to know how to relax. Again, the teacher or counselor should encourage the parents to practice with their child at home.

From Bloomquist, 1996

Zip My Lip

John Taylor's intervention, "zip my lip, turn around, and leave," can be effective in de-escalating aggressive interactions (Taylor, 1994, 2006). This simple rhyme, when practiced often, can help children remember to stop, leave, and find something else to do until they calm down. With young children, it's important to practice this when they are not upset or angry. Like with muscle memory, the more the children practice these steps, the chances are better that when getting upset, they will zip their lips, turn around, and leave the situation.

Three, Two, One Card (Grades 4–6)

Three, Two, One Card is an easy monitoring tool to use. It allows the teacher to quickly monitor students' moods throughout the school day. The teacher puts the numbers 3, 2, 1 on a 2 × 8 card and asks children which number best represents their mood at the time they are shown the card. The number three represents happy; two represents not sure; and one represents angry. If the children answer two or one, the teacher can take time to talk with them or encourage them; if they seem pretty upset, they are allowed to go to their calm-down area until they feel calmer. The children should be given verbal praise or a token for following the teacher's directions. Like most interventions, the parents are encouraged to practice this activity at home with their child.

If students present significant difficulty calming down, it may be helpful to have them practice appropriate calming self-talk in conjunction with physical soothing activities (young children could gently be rocked; older children could be provided a pile of foam pillows or similar arranged areas in the company of a calm and accepting adult, if possible). One of the authors, when teaching middle school, had a couch at the back of his room with pillows. He found this an ideal area for affected students needing time by themselves when agitated or highly distracted. For extremely angry affected children, often you will find that simply being by themselves may not be enough.

It's important that this process be done throughout the school day and not just when children seem angry. The more children practice these interventions the better they will be at identifying unhappy feelings before they become a problem. The teacher needs to see these interventions as a proactive procedure to lessen angry outbursts in class. These interventions can be very helpful teaching children to begin to identify when they are becoming upset and model a socially appropriate way to let a caretaker know how they feel.

Take 5

Take 5 (a technique created by an unknown author) is a great tool for helping children deal with their anger. It provides, through a visual example (see Figure 5.1, Take 5 Hand), steps to practice dealing with

Figure 5.1

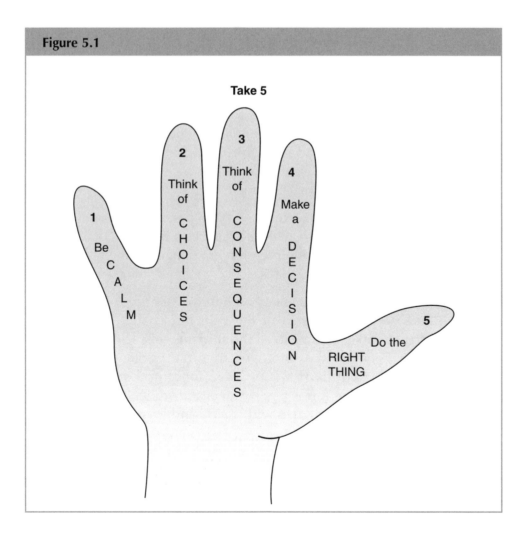

anger or other actions that can get children in trouble. It works best for latency-age children and early adolescents.

As illustrated in Figure 5.1, children are shown a picture of an open hand with five fingers. On each finger is a reminder: (1) be *calm*, (2) think of *choices*, (3) think of *consequences*, (4) make a *decision*, and (5) do the *right thing*. Children can practice these steps at home, in the counselor's office, or in the classroom. After time, children are able to go through these five self-directed steps without a reminder or looking at the visual cue.

It can be put on 8×11 copy paper or a 3×5 card and posted inside the students' desks. Like all behavioral interventions, it works best when the parents practice this intervention with their child at home.

Recommended Monitoring Steps

1. For the first three weeks a new intervention is introduced, the school counselor should observe and support students learning the new behavior by spending time in the classroom, at least weekly if not more, to assess their understanding and compliance to the intervention. The counselor should ask the teacher to implement the intervention with children so the counselor can observe their performance.

2. The counselor should meet twice a week with the teacher to review data on the progress the children have made over the three weeks. The data should be used to determine if further observations and training are necessary. Further consultations should occur until the children's anger outbursts diminish.

3. The counselor should also meet with the parents to review the data on their child's progress with the teacher's interventions. Recommendations for further intervention or changes to the intervention process can be made at this time.

4. The counselor should also meet with the students weekly to review the data on their progress in the behavior change process. It is important to take the time to let the students see the data that show that their behavior has improved in some visual, concrete way. Intervention Central (www.interventioncentral.org) has many student-monitoring forms that teachers and students can customize and use to monitor progress with charts and graphs.

5. If the children are on medication, the counselor should get a release of information from the parents to speak with the doctor about any possible side effects from the medication. Children with ADHD can

develop comorbid disorders (depression, anxiety, oppositional-defiant disorder [ODD]) that can impact the effectiveness of any medication treatment. Often, medication needs must be adjusted numerous times to find the appropriate dosage for the most benefit. If the medication does not seem to have a positive effect on the child's ability to focus, attend, and control behavior, this information needs to be shared with the parents and doctor. Last, comorbid disorders can cause significant behavioral problems for children, even though the ADHD medication may be addressing the core ADHD symptoms. This is important to note because teachers will often find children are still agitated and uncooperative in class, but many times, these behaviors reflect a mood disorder or ODD and are not necessarily related to their ADHD diagnosis.

6. Children with ADHD often will benefit from individual counseling to assess and address possible risk factors that may be impacting on behavioral and academic interventions. Sometimes anger is a window into deeper issues that call for individual sessions in the counselor's office.

Middle School and High School

When children reach middle school and high school age, they generally understand that they have more control over their emotions and what happens to them. Most of the time, they see themselves as being more in control of events and situations, whether it is at school or at home. Consequently, children at this stage in development are more capable of self-regulating and self-monitoring their behavior when they feel that they do have some control over their situation.

When they feel cornered and feel that they have no choices, they will often lash out behaviorally because they have lost that sense of control. All adolescents struggle with these control issues, and adolescents with ADHD are even more challenged because of their disorder, but they still can temper their anger when directly taught self-help strategies. At this age, they can and should be expected to become more of a participant in their treatment.

As adolescents, they want their complaints listened to, they want respect, and they want to have choices as they move toward greater independence and more self-regulation. They are very self-aware and are more sensitive to "not making a fool of themselves" in front of their peers. As they mature, they don't want to be bullied by peers or adults. They want a say in how they are treated both by their peers and the adults in their lives. As adults, we sometimes forget that childhood is a process for change and learning. Few people emerge full-grown like Athena from the head of Zeus, but all grow slowly and gradually, taking step after step toward independent judgment and adulthood. Affected young people will make mistakes, and how we deal with them during these challenging times can make a big difference in their acceptance of our advice and guidance.

Some of the interventions focused on adolescents are similar to those discussed for younger children; however, adolescents will be expected to be more proactive and involved in the intervention's implementation. There are, however, some associated disorders commonly seen with ADHD that can make cooperation and follow-through more difficult with affected adolescents. First, the adolescent with ADHD can be impacted by anxiety, oppositional and defiant behaviors, and depression. For a minority of affected students, you also will see obsessive-compulsive traits and cognitive processing disorders, such as auditory processing disorders. Consequently, the counselor and teacher need to recognize that sometimes these interventions will not be as successful as one would hope. Some of these young people will need additional support to address school-based behaviors.

Coping Self-Talk

As with younger children, demonstrating and teaching self-talk can be very helpful in tempering angry outbursts and unhappy feelings with older students. Often, older students are more receptive to this technique because they experience success with it and verbalize this awareness to the counselor or teacher. They are able to practice more on their own and recognize that it *can* help them not become upset so quickly.

Teachers or the counselor can provide students examples of coping self-talk to say when they find themselves becoming upset. First, however, the teacher or counselor needs to take a few minutes to explain to students that self-talk involves saying things to oneself to help calm down. Second, examples need to be provided, such as the ones below suggested by Dr. Bloomquist (1996, p. 156).

- "Take it easy."
- "Stay cool."
- "Take some deep breaths." (The teacher needs to demonstrate deep and slow breathing so the child understands what to do.)
- "It's okay if I'm not good at this."
- "I am sad Bobby doesn't want to play with me, but many other kids like to play with me."
- "I'll just try my hardest."
- "Try not to give up."
- "I need to relax."

After students seem to understand the concept, it's important to remind the teacher that the students should be encouraged to practice and use calming self-talk several times during the school day. Students can also practice this intervention in the counselor's office or at home. We have found when reinforced and practiced at home, it can provide the student with more *real-time* practice opportunities. Yet as any parents who have raised an adolescent know, adolescent children are not always open to the advice of parents. However, if the parents provide positive reinforcement by pointing out when their child has used the technique, it can be a surprisingly powerful reinforcer.

We have found that this activity, to point out a few examples, can be practiced just before leaving for recess or break (30 second reminder), when transitioning to an activity the teacher knows may be challenging to the student (quiet reminder to use calm self-talk words when frustrated), or on a field trip where an affected student will need reminders on ways to deal with angry feelings. High school age students seem to embrace this strategy when it is discussed or practiced in the privacy of the counselor's office more than being discussed by a teacher in front of their peers. Adolescents generally are resistant to in-class discussions centering on *their* behaviors. The authors have found that seeing counselors in their office generally is the best climate to practice this intervention with adolescents.

The benefit of this intervention is that it can help students find a new way to deal with angry or unhappy emotions. It's important that this intervention be practiced on a regular basis and not used only after the student has had an outburst or emotional breakdown. Affected students need more reminders and more practice because they don't learn from their mistakes as well as unaffected young adults. However, it does require more time commitment from the teacher and counselor than other interventions used in a school setting, but the payoff, learning a lifelong coping skill, is worth the time and effort.

Self-Monitoring Sheet on Anger-Coping Procedures

Self-monitoring requires student cooperation. Generally, this intervention is recommended for students who seem motivated to work on ways to help them with their anger. It requires the children to keep a log and write down steps they are going to do to help them deal with their anger. Bloomquist (1996, p. 164) presents six steps from his "Coping With Anger Worksheet."

1. Children write down what problem or event is making them angry.

2. Children write down the body, thought, and actions that tell them that they are experiencing anger. (e.g., "My heart was pounding," "I would like to hit him," or "I was clinching my fist and yelling at him.")

3. Children write down what they can do to relax their body (deep breathing, coping self-talk).

4. Children write down what coping self-talk they can use to control their thoughts. (e.g., "I will take some deep breaths and try to relax my body," or "I will walk away from the situation.")

5. Children write down what effective actions they can take to deal with the situation or solve the problem. (e.g., "I will spend time with another friend," or "I will talk with him later when I am more relaxed and not so upset.")

6. The children rate themselves on a four-point scale describing how successfully they coped with their anger.

   a. Coping With Anger Rating (circles one)
      o Didn't try to cope with anger at all
      o Sort of tried to cope with anger, but it didn't really work
      o Tried hard to cope with anger, but it didn't really work
      o Tried hard to cope with anger, and it worked

Bloomquist (1996) recommends that children go through these steps when they are feeling angry, but it's also okay to use them after the fact as well. It can be a learning tool to evaluate the children's progress in coping with anger as they collect data over time. Tracking progress in this manner may help them learn to recognize patterns of behavior linked to certain situations, events, or people that lead to having difficulty coping with their anger. Being able to recognize patterns in their own behaviors helps students feel like they can control what happens to them, and once they recognize their own behavioral triggers, they can learn on their own how to avoid them.

The authors have found this process very motivating because students can see from the data that they can improve. The counselor can set up a system where the student can track their own behaviors on charts or rubrics, either developed by the student or obtained from a Web site like www.interventioncentral.org. The counselor can set up a reward system (late latency and early adolescence) for keeping the data in a log and bringing it to the counseling session. Although, once students can see progress based on the data, often a reward system is no longer necessary. Older adolescents respond best to adult reinforcement—positive affirmations that tell them that they are capable of making progress and improving their behaviors.

This intervention needs to be done in a counseling session and should not be seen as a classroom intervention. It requires a number of steps to be successful.

- Determining if the children are ready for this intervention (e.g., not too defensive, old enough)
- Helping the children recognize signs when they are angry (e.g., "My face turned red," "Telling myself I am dumb," and yelling or crying)
- Teaching the children how to relax
- Teaching the children to use coping self-talk
- Modeling coping with anger
- Monitoring and setting up formal anger-coping procedures

The reader is encouraged to look at Bloomquist's (1996) excellent book, *Skills Training for Children With Behavior Disorders,* for more discussion on this specific intervention.

Time-Out

Time-out is an intervention where students are asked to spend a period of time by themselves. It is mainly effective with children 4 to 12 years of age. Consequently, it should be used selectively with middle school and high school students.

Purpose of Time-Out

The purpose of a time-out period is not to punish but to help students calm down until they are able to join a classroom activity. When talking about time-out in middle and high school, we suggest that it be viewed as a voluntarily agreed on *contractual agreement* between the students and the teacher. It should be seen by both the teacher and students as a means of addressing those moments when the students need time by themselves to regroup and calm down. It is important that students also be given the option of putting themselves in time-out when they find themselves getting very upset. The students, while in time-out, could have access to soothing materials, such as headphones with soft music (white noise). Some classrooms have blankets, stuffed animals, and the like, which are great materials for enhancing sensual soothing and recentering upset or angry children. Time-out, like other coping skills, is a positive choice over yelling or running outside the room. Adults use this process in any number of situations (i.e., the husband or wife going into the home office or garage to calm down to get away from an angry spouse). Like conflicts in a marriage, it is meant only as a temporary means to keep tempers down, not as an avenue for avoiding a problem or dodging classwork.

This contract needs to be clear and seen as reasonable by both teacher and students. The goals for both teacher and students should be to help the students find a way to regulate themselves and maintain a working relationship between the teacher and students, and it should not be seen as a win-lose process but rather a win-win process.

We suggest that there be a limited number (our recommendation is not more than three) of times middle school students can use time-outs during the school day. By setting a limit of three times, students are forced to decide if they can calm down without using a time-out slot. It makes students think twice before using a time-out slot. By setting a limit of times, it can be used as reinforcement for students to practice their coping self-talk and other techniques. At the beginning, however, it is sometimes necessary to start off without a limited number of time-out slots to provide the emotionally volatile students immediate support.

Time-Out in Junior High and High School

The time-out intervention is more difficult to set up in a junior high or high school setting, but not impossible. It requires a meeting between the counselor and the students' teachers to set up the parameters. Obviously, with a number of class changes in junior high and high school, the method and process would need to be adjusted accordingly, with frequent communication between the counselor and all the students' teachers. One of the authors was a school counselor in a middle school and used this intervention successfully on a number of affected students. He met with the students weekly and went over their progress. A meeting had taken place with the students' teachers, and it was agreed that when upset, students could go to the back of the room and not participate in class activities until they felt less angry. After a relatively short period of time, the students did not generally need this special arrangement and were able to do better by seeing their counselor and continuing to practice their self-talk intervention.

Catch Them Being Good

It is integral that the teacher not bypass the greatest opportunity for shaping and reinforcing appropriate behavior when working with children with ADHD: *Catch them being good*. It's imperative that this step not be missed. Experts agree that although many teachers are aware of the powerful effects of praise, they often under use it (Conroy, Sutherland, Snyder, & Marsh, 2008). Children with ADHD respond best to immediate reinforcement, so the sooner the appropriate behavior is positively recognized the more effective the reinforcement becomes. The reinforcement shouldn't be a token but a simple, sincere, and specific comment. Specific praise occurs when the teacher specifies the target behavior reinforced within the statement.

- "Bobby, I like the way you turned in your math paper today. I know it's hard to always remember."
- "Sally, thank you for walking away from Alice when you felt your-self getting mad. It's hard to stop and walk away in times like this, and I wanted to let you know I noticed. Thank you."
- "Tom, I saw Ryan want to talk to you during the test; you did great by ignoring him until I could get to his desk. I know this is hard to do when it's a friend. Thanks."

By evaluating the appropriate behavior, and naming it, students are able to recognize directly what they did that was right. Saying "good boy" is not definitive and students are often confused about what made them "good" for that second. Praise and recognition of appropriate behavior is so important because the formula for real change comes from establishing and reinforcing the building of a positive relationship between students and teacher, as well as shaping the behaviors that will support lifelong social-skills development. In general, teachers should offer praise statements more often than corrective statements. For example, Good and Grouws (1977) recommend that teachers strive to achieve and maintain a ratio of four or five positive statements to one corrective statement. The counselor needs to emphasize strongly that no technique or intervention is going to bring about real long-term change in children if trusting and caring relationships are not estab-lished with the teacher.

Argumentative Behaviors

Children with ADHD frequently come across as oppositional and argumentative. A majority of children with ADHD-HI will be diagnosed with ODD. However, what at times seem like arguments rather are anx-ious, impulsive students who have great difficulty regulating their actions and words.

It's important to try to separate ODD behaviors from impulsive behaviors that often are masking a fear of failure or failing in front of peers or diffi-culty regulating their words or actions.

Children with ADHD often have difficulty tempering their words and actions when faced with the following situations.

- When asked to do something they don't like doing
- When asked to stop doing something that they enjoy to do something less enjoyable

- When asked to stop doing something that they may not be aware they are doing (e.g., tapping their feet, scribbling on their workbook, getting up and walking around the room when the teacher is lecturing, and forgetting to put away their books before going to recess)

ODD behaviors are generally pervasive and chronic across different environmental settings. Unlike ODD, argumentative behavior is often situational in scope and is generally manifested when affected children are asked to do something that they are uncomfortable doing. The underlying theme is not just that "I don't want to do it" but that it is something that they find uncomfortable and may be anxious about doing it.

Students with ADHD can be defiant and argumentative. This is especially true for teens who are comparatively more inattentive and impulsive (Barkley & Robin, 2008). In fact, considering their traits and interactions with caretakers throughout their childhood, they can develop a pattern of behavior where they have a negative emotional reaction to teachers or parents "hovering" or making "demands" of them. Unfortunately, the response of caretakers is often to become more coercive and demanding. Barkley and Robin (2008) write the following:

> When a child can't sustain attention, acts impulsively, and can't sit still—characteristically, not just occasionally—parents (and teachers) are likely to end up issuing more commands, to supervise more closely, and to be more critical, creating disproportionately more negative than positive interactions with the child. (p. 57)

Consequently, counselors should alert teachers about this possibility and encourage them to be more aware of this pattern of interaction. Also, encourage teachers to put more effort into identifying their level of responsibility toward promoting argumentative behaviors with the affected student. Once teachers recognize and keep track of the number of negative and positive interactions that they have with a student in a day, they can make an effort to change this pattern of behavior.

Suggestions to Address Argumentative Behaviors

- Alert students before transitions that the transition is about to occur and that there will be a change in focus (e.g., stopping math and starting English, stopping independent reading and opening up the math book).

- Remind students that their goal for the day is to ask for clarification if confused but not to argue. Model for students how to ask for clarification appropriately, as some students may struggle with the ability to form questions or ask for clarification. This verbal reminder and modeling needs to occur throughout the day, not just at the beginning of the class period.

- Give students frequent verbal praise when they are observed following the teacher's directions without arguing. Again, providing positive, direct verbal reinforcement when the student is caught being compliant cannot be over stated. Providing descriptive reinforcement creates clarity for students on what appropriate behaviors are and provides strong relationship-building material for the teacher and students. It also minimizes the students' feeling victimized when they realize that they do have appropriate behaviors and they are recognized by others. Children with ADHD generally have less success with positive reinforcement than unaffected children; however, praise and concrete rewards go a long way in providing the teacher positive tools and positive interactions when dealing with students.

- Use a reward or token system for following directions and not arguing with the teacher. (This is most effective with latency-age children. Adolescents generally respond better to contractual arrangements that come from honest dialogue between the teacher and children.)

- Assess whether students are more interested in winning or resolving the problem. The counselor can be helpful in separating ODD behavior from ADHD traits. If children are more interested in winning or getting the teacher mad than discussing the problem, talking generally doesn't help with this ODD behavior. Immediate consequences are required, rather than *talking*, because children at that point are not interested in resolving any problems.

Oppositional Versus Unintentional Behavior

Children with ADHD often are seen as refusing to do what they are asked; where in fact, often it's not oppositional behavior but difficulty *remembering to remember.* It is very important to separate oppositional behavior from forgetfulness.

Oppositional or noncompliant behaviors are purposeful and willful by nature, whereas, forgetfulness or distractions are unintentional by nature. Unfortunately, it is sometimes hard separating these behaviors in the classroom. However, to assure fairness, it is important to find ways to make this distinction.

Suggestions to Distinguish Oppositional From Unintentional Behavior

- The teacher stands next to students' desks and waits for them to start on the assigned task. Children with ADHD are generally not self-starters and might need a teacher or classroom aide to give them assurance on how to start an assignment. This is especially true when asked to do unfamiliar, difficult, or belaboring activities. Even a high school student will need this level of support at times to assure them that they are on the right track and are doing the right thing.
- The teacher intermittently goes to students' desks to refocus or redirect them back to their work if observed not working. Quiet reminders that explicitly specify what they should be doing serve to reinforce them enough to continue to work. Generally compliant children will return to the task, whereas noncompliant children will refuse or argue back.
- The teacher needs to quickly assess whether refusal to do an assignment is because of the difficulty of the work or the anxiety that comes from facing a new and unknown task without appropriate models. For many students with ADHD, writing assignments can be very difficult, and without proper prewriting activities and scaffolds, they will resist starting worksheets or essays (see Chapter 4).

Suggestions for Dealing With Noncompliant Behaviors

- Relationships change behavior, not rules or techniques alone. If a teacher loses children's respect, little can be done to help turn around noncompliant children.
- Showing respect to the individual as a person provides the foundation for a positive relationship. Recognizing the needs of students and agreeing with students create a situation where an argument cannot continue. Responding respectfully with a comment like, "I can see how you might think this assignment is stupid. I know it is hard and the directions seem confusing," creates a situation where students can no longer argue because you have agreed with them. This provides a step-off point to find out what underlying situation is truly driving the argument.
- Positive reinforcement of compliant behaviors is critical for establishing a platform on which to begin to address ODD behaviors. Catch them being good and specifically defining what the appropriate behaviors are can go a long way in developing compliant behaviors and respect.

- Younger students respond to tokens or rewards, whereas adolescents respond best to behavioral contracts mutually agreed on, choices within the classroom context, as well as honest, sincere, specific praise.
- Adolescents are very sensitive about what their peers think of them. When approaching noncompliant behavior, it's best to do it privately or respectfully. Put-downs, power struggles, and snide remarks often backfire. No one wins, teacher or student.
- Sometimes, when classroom interventions have failed, it is necessary for the teacher to bring in the school counselor, administrator, or the parents to address the children's behavior.

Dealing with noncompliance or refusal to do schoolwork can be difficult; however, when teachers try to identify the cause for the behavior and have a positive relationship and respect for students' feelings, they can go a long way in bringing about compliant behaviors. The authors would recommend Dr. Taylor's (2001) excellent book, *From Defiance to Cooperation: Real Solutions for Transforming the Angry, Defiant, Discouraged Child*, for further discussion on this topic.

Hyperkinetic and Fidgety Behaviors

In our conversations with teachers, one behavioral trait that often comes up is how to deal with affected children's hyperkinetic and fidgety behaviors when they impact other children's learning. Even children on medication will continue to move in their seats or be fidgety: medication often reduces these behaviors, but seldom eliminates them.

Hyperkinetic behaviors are more pronounced in younger children than in adolescents; however, both age groups have difficulty monitoring or self-regulating their body activity. High school students generally are fidgety more than hyperactive. They will be found bouncing their legs, crisscrossing their legs back and forth, tapping a pencil on the desk top, or doodling on the desk top.

These behaviors, though not seriously dangerous or destructive, can be distracting to a teacher and classmates, but rarely affect children's ability to learn. In fact, many students with ADHD report that they can attend and focus better when they are moving, doodling, or fidgeting than when trying to stay still.

There are some simple strategies that can help *minimize* some of these movements, but before putting a lot of time and energy into modifying these behaviors, it is important to recognize that it is usually the teacher who has a greater problem with them than other students in the classroom. These strategies may help reduce but will not totally stop fidgety behaviors.

Suggestions to Minimize Disruptive Behaviors

- Try to ignore minor body movement (e.g., one leg on the chair top, leg bouncing, tapping feet, rolling a pencil back and forth in the palm of a hand, and chewing a pencil eraser). If not too loud or too disruptive, ignore it until you are done presenting the lesson, giving a direction, or setting up a classroom assignment. Then go to their desk and quietly remind them to stop. This can be done verbally or through a silent signal. Children are rarely aware that they are doing it. Also, remember that even though children may be fidgety, it doesn't mean they are not listening and not learning. However, many times directing children to "stop" only temporarily stops the behavior because the underlying condition makes it nearly impossible for affected children to stop fiddling or moving around at their desks for long.
- Students can also be allowed to hold or fondle a piece of string, yarn, or a small soft cloth while seated at their desks.
- For younger children, tennis balls on the bottom of their chair legs can help minimize noise and movement from children who move their seats around a lot.
- A specialized cushion, like a Disco Sit, allows young children to move their bottom in their seat without disrupting the children around them. The specialized cushions can be found at www.abilitations.com. Also, some no-cost alternatives that can accomplish the same thing are a small sofa pillow or stadium cushion for the children to sit on, or allowing the students to sit on their own jacket.
- Keeping busy hands busy in appropriate ways can avoid problems with movement and the inappropriate touching of objects and other students. Giving children a replacement object to hold helps redirect their need to move, such as a cushy ball or other fidget toys to play with while waiting during a classroom transition or while standing in line. Preferential seating is essential for fidgety students. These students may need to sit somewhere that they can move around and not distract others (the very back or at a separate seating area) but still be able to see the front when the teacher is giving specific directions.

Recess and Free Time Are Especially Difficult

Unstructured time (recess) and in-class free time (transitioning between classes in middle or high school) can often be a difficult times for students with ADHD. They often have difficulty estimating time, can become highly distracted, and in less-structured environments, can present elevated hyperkinetic and impulsive behaviors.

These children seem to get in trouble more often than their classmates during these unstructured times. Consequently, a school counselor can be especially supportive in providing affected students with suggestions for keeping out of trouble and not being tardy.

Suggestions to Deal With Free Time

Recess

Students with ADHD should never leave the room without a plan. They are not good at sequencing and planning their free time, so it is important to touch base with them just before leaving for recess. School-age children (K–6) need the teacher to review with them what to do when they find themselves upset or unsure of what to do next (where to go when upset, who to talk to if angry, what to do if all the balls are already taken). The teacher may also want to assign a class buddy to remind them that it's time to line up from recess when the bell rings.

Free Time

Affected children need close monitoring and reminders during in-class free time. With lack of structure, they often can become overly excited and start running, yelling, and the like. They need to have a menu of activities to be involved in during the free time to help them maintain control. They also need to understand that the teacher will ask them to sit at their quiet space if they become too disruptive (tokens and verbal praise can help reinforce appropriate in-class behaviors).

- Middle school and high school students also need additional reminders and a plan to deal with transitioning and free time. Lunch time can be a rewarding and fun time, but also a setting for trouble. It's a time and place where the students can relax and talk with friends, but it's also a place where they can cause others around them to become angry because of their poor choice of words or impulsive actions. Junior high and high school students often find themselves tardy to class because of poor time management and high distractibility.
- School-age children often respond well to concrete monitoring sheets that go with them at recess and are returned when recess is over. One that the authors have found helpful is a 2 × 8 sheet of colored paper with numbers 3, 2, 1 on the front. Three is "good," two is "fair," and one is "poor," in terms of meeting the recess goals for

the student. The students give the monitoring slip to the recess teacher, and the teacher signs off on their behavior when recess is over, and this is returned to the teacher for the appropriate reward or consequence.

- Middle school age or high school age students can benefit from visual reminders (stickers), placed were they can easily be seen, meaning "get to class" or "stop talking and start walking." Students can also use the alarms in their cell phones, watches, or iPods to remind them to get to class or start walking toward class before the bell rings. (However, this intervention may not be an option if the school doesn't allow cell phones on during school hours.) A class-mate can also help remind affected students to "stop talking and start walking." The authors have found that these simple reminders can help those students who struggle with time management. These are effective self-monitoring tools that can help students keep on track and remember to remember.

Interruptions in Class

Teachers often bring students who just can't stop interrupting or blurting out in class to a counselor's attention. It can be annoying to a teacher who is trying to cover a content area and is constantly being interrupted by having to attend to these students.

These students have greater difficulty with cognitive or behavioral impulsivity (saying or doing whatever comes to their mind without stopping to think about the consequences) than classmates their age. ADHD by definition is developmental delay in inhibition. Affected students can be more successful, but it would be unreasonable to believe their disruptive behaviors will completely disappear.

Suggestions to Minimize Interruptions

- Quietly remind students at the beginning of class that they need to try to raise their hands before asking or commenting on a question. However, as mentioned in Chapter 2, affected children feel if they don't "say it now, they may forget." They also have great difficulty with delayed gratification. "I need to know now!"
- Let students know they will be called on only a certain number of times during a particular lesson. Give students this same number of paper clips or other objects that can help remind the students how many times they will be called on. In a small group setting, they give the teacher one object for each comment. When they are out of

objects, they have used up their opportunities to speak. This can sometimes help students monitor themselves better and help them be more selective on when they will raise their hand.

- Highly impulsive children can be seated closer to the front of the classroom where the teacher can provide verbal and nonverbal reminders to raise their hand before asking a question. For example, the teacher can let children know before the lesson begins that, "I will call on you when I see your hand up, so be careful to raise your hand if you have a question," or "If I place my hand on your desk, it's a reminder that you talked out and need to raise your hand before I can call on you."

- Stickers on the students' desks or work areas can help remind students to raise their hand. The teacher will need to remind students throughout the school day to practice looking at their reminder stickers.

- Teachers who provide numerous opportunities to respond as a class, in small groups, or individually find increases in on-task behaviors and correct responses and have fewer in-class disruptions (Sutherland, Alder, & Gunter, 2003). Allowing students numerous opportunities to talk to each other will reduce children's need to blurt out.

- Middle school and high school students often are better at regulating outbursts than younger children; however, they also are sometimes disconnected from the class discussion. Without frequent opportunities to respond and engage in discussion in class, many times, they will be either distracting another student or "in their own world."

Hums, Whistles, or Other Noises in Class

Students with ADHD can often be found humming, whistling, or making other noises at their desks while working. These vocal sounds can help these students focus and attend to their work or remain more focused when reading by blocking out other noises; however, for the classmates around these students, it can be disruptive. Just like affected students will sometimes move to help stay focused, they also will be observed making vocal sounds to help with focusing and selective attention. It's important to remember that in the majority of cases, this "bad" behavior is not willful or purposeful. The teacher should allow the student to move away from others when it becomes too distracting for others. Punishment is not an appropriate strategy to deal with this issue.

Suggestions to Address Vocal Disruptions in Class

- Preferential seating so the teacher can closely monitor and gently remind students if they are too loud.
- Allow students to move to another part of the room to complete the assignment, away from other students who may be affected by the noise.
- Get permission to talk with children's doctors if the vocal sounds seem like they might represent vocal tics, which may be an indication of Tourette syndrome (e.g., recurrent grunts, snorts, whistles, moans, sniffles, throat clearing, or sucking in air). Sometimes, ADHD medications can trigger or exacerbate vocal and/or motor tics, so your observations could be important for the treating physician to be aware of.

Parent Participation

Lack of parent participation is a frequent, contentious discussion in school staff rooms. When parent involvement is lacking, it is that much more difficult to change behaviors with disruptive and oppositional students.

However, blaming the parents is not helpful. It diminishes the possibility of a positive trusting relationship with the parents, which is necessary to work as a team. Blame often originates from frustration and desperation to find some solution to deal with difficult students. Generally, the parents are equally frustrated with their child's behaviors and will want to blame the school or the teachers for the problems that their child faces. Both find comfort in finding someone or something that can explain the child's disruptive and difficult behaviors.

It's important to appreciate that by the time this child reaches the third grade, the parents will have devoted a considerable amount of time and energy into attempting to understand and manage their child's behavior. Parents of affected children attend more school conferences, doctor appointments, and principal meetings and resolve more conflicts between their child and neighbors, police, and siblings and often are dealing with ongoing spousal differences over "best parenting" than are parents of unaffected children. Often, by the time they are asked to attend *another school meeting* about their child, they are totally defeated. Over many battles and a sense of failure, parents can develop what Barkley (2000) refers to as *learned helplessness*, an attitude where a parent feels that no matter what they do, nothing seems to work.

The counselor, therefore, needs to provide the parents validation for their efforts, understanding of their situation, and support for their child at school.

The parents need to know that there is an advocate for them and their child at school—an advocate that can appreciate their pain, relate to their frustration, and go to bat for their child when needed. No school person is more trained or in a better position to take on this important role than the school counselor. The counselor can be a lifeline for the child, teacher, and parents. Like the child and parents, the teacher also needs the counselor's support in getting the parents more involved in their child's education. This task is not easy or conflict free, but it is critical. The team approach is very important if any long-term progress is going to occur.

Suggestions to Address Parent Participation

- The counselor should help establish an open and supportive communication between the child's teachers and the parents. An important goal should be to recognize the teachers' and parents' temperaments, history of their relationship, and their perceptions as to their role in the child's treatment.
- The counselor should be available by e-mail or phone to communicate with the parents. Close communication is especially critical when the child is in crisis.
- The counselor should ask for regular meetings with the parents to discuss the child's diagnosis and how it is affecting their schooling. Education on ADHD for the parents is a critical goal if parent participation is going to improve (see Chapter 3, Parental and Family Assessment Is Important.) The parents need to see that their involvement is absolutely necessary for the betterment of their child.
- The counselor should assess the parent-child relationship to determine the level of support that parents can give the teacher in setting boundaries, consequences, and rewards.

In closing, helping the parents understand ADHD, providing them positive support, helping them find energy and strategies to reduce their family tension, and convincing them that they play an integral role in the educational success of their child can help the team realize improved outcomes for the child.

THE TEACHER MAY HAVE TO MAKE SOME CHANGES TOO

Last, the classroom teachers often can help the situation by making some minor changes in their interactions with the children. At times, it is necessary for the school counselor to remind teachers and other school staff that school is about children and learning, not about adults getting what they want. Children with ADHD will need more reminders; they will need preferential seating; and they will probably need a *grace period* for turning in homework or class assignments. The teacher will need to take the time to tease out noncompliant or indifference toward doing the schoolwork and ADHD traits, such as forgetting to turn in completed work. Providing these accommodations is not optional. As discussed in earlier chapters, such accommodations are not enabling but are fair and appropriate interventions for students with ADHD.

Summary

Intervening on behalf of students with ADHD can often be very challenging, but it is integral to the success of an affected student. We have attempted to outline those areas most often brought to counselors' attention and have provided suggestions that can be successfully implemented in a school setting. We have focused on anger- and disruptive-based behaviors not because all children with ADHD exhibit them but because these are the behaviors that most often bring these children to the school counselor's attention. We understand that there are many other areas where students with ADHD struggle, but these seem to be the most problematic and can often get in the way of a successful school experience.

Hopefully, the reader has been provided enough examples to take these strategies and information from the other chapters to help affected students move beyond problem behaviors that can plague them every day.

6 What Teachers Should Know About Medication

David Rosenthal, MD

A mother, after being confronted by a pharmacist's wife, came to the doctor's office feeling angry, embarrassed, and hurt. When she had picked up her child's medication at the pharmacy, the pharmacist's wife had told her, "I wouldn't put my child on Ritalin, and you should think twice about giving your child Ritalin." The mother had left feeling attacked and guilt-ridden.

Medicating children for ADHD continues to be controversial, especially in light of the dramatic increase in the number of prescriptions for stimulant medications being written in the past few years across the United States. Peter Breggin (1998), an outspoken physician and writer, advocates stopping the current trend in medicating children with ADHD. He argues that not only is Ritalin uncalled for on many occasions but that it can have serious side effects that are not brought to the parent's attention. He suggests that teachers, much like parents, feel pressured to find shortcuts for dealing with the disruptive and fidgety children and that support groups and drug companies, for both political and financial reasons, are misleading them. The consequence is that more and more American children are now being medicated for ADHD.

The media regularly add to the controversy by producing headlines that are designed to attract attention and do not always accurately transmit scientific facts. This example is from the Detroit News: *Michigan ranks third in nation in prescribing Ritalin: Some say schools turn to medication to control students. Ritalin's routine use raises alarm over diagnosis, goals. Use of Ritalin in schools nearly out of control* (1998).

However, according to a report by the American Medical Association's Council of Scientific Affairs (Goldman, Genel, Bezman, & Slanetz, 1998), overprescription of drugs to treat the disorder is not widespread. Dr. Richard Nakamura, acting director of the National Institute of Mental Health, in his testimony before the Committee on Government Reform, United States House of Representatives (September 26, 2002), stated that

> little evidence of overdiagnosis of ADHD or overprescription of stimulant medications has been verified in research. Indeed, fewer children (2% to 3% of school-age children) are being treated for ADHD than suffer from it. Treatment rates are much lower for girls, minorities, and children receiving care through public service systems. (Nakamura, 2002)

Parents may find themselves wondering how they can possibly decide whether to medicate their children when doctors themselves can't seem to agree. School counselors, like parents, will often express reservations around the issue of medicating children for ADHD.

This chapter is not intended to promote or to dispute the claims of others about the role of medication in the treatment of ADHD but rather to educate school counselors on the current medications used in the treatment of ADHD, the limitations of medication, and parental concerns that counselors should be aware of. The authors recognize that medication alone will not address all the challenges experienced by children with ADHD in a school setting, and "without the inclusion of a range of non-pharmaceutical interventions and techniques, medication alone in many cases is doomed, if not to fail entirely, at least to prove disappointing" (Garber, Garber, & Spizman, 1996, p. 5). The authors believe that even though medication should not be seen as a *magical pill* that will correct all ADHD behaviors, we would be remiss in not pointing out that research has shown that medication coupled with behavior intervention is more effective in reducing or modifying many of the problems associated with ADHD than either medication or behavioral approaches alone. Consequently, our strong belief is that medication has an important role to play in the treatment of ADHD.

Dr. Rosenthal overviews the importance of ongoing communication, with signed permission, between the school counselor, the teacher, and the child's doctor once a child is started on medication. A young child can spend four to six hours in school, and a counselor's feedback on the child's behaviors while on medication is very important in helping the doctor to measure the effectiveness of the medication and to assess the need for changes in dosage.

Dr. Rosenthal looks at some common side effects from ADHD medications and feels that a school counselor's awareness of these possible side effects is important to assure the most effective treatment of the child's condition. The information provided in this chapter should give guidance and answer many of your questions and concerns.

SHOULD MY CHILD BE ON MEDICATION?

As just noted, the decision about whether or not to put a child on medication is a very difficult decision for many parents to make. For some, this difficulty centers on guilt. As discussed in earlier chapters, parents may be falsely concluding that their child's ADHD diagnosis is somehow their fault, either because they feel they gave their child bad genes or because they feel that they did something wrong in raising their child. This guilt tends to increase when the parents are asked to approve subjecting their child to what, in their minds, might be a potentially dangerous medication.

It doesn't help matters when their child, who may already be upset about getting the message that he or she is somehow flawed, may be vigorously opposed to being on a strict medication regimen. Or it may be that the parents are already concerned about the stigma associated with a *mental* diagnosis, now compounded by the idea that, as several parents have put it, "it must really be bad if they think my child needs medication."

Despite these concerns, the most common medications used to treat ADHD, while not necessarily completely benign, do tend to be very well tolerated with a minimum of side effects for the majority of children. Additionally, studies support the idea that, in most cases, using medication is the single most important intervention that parents can make in managing their child's core ADHD symptoms. Studies that have compared stimulants with psychosocial treatment have consistently found greater efficacy with stimulants. However, this in no way negates the importance of all of the other behavioral and environmental intervention strategies suggested in this book. We are suggesting, however, that a combined approach may offer the best results for your child.

It is always important to remember that despite concerns about stigma and medication side effects, a decision to *not* treat ADHD may have significant negative consequences for a child, not just in terms of ongoing problems with school performance but with the multiple social and secondary psychological problems that can occur if impulsivity and socially inappropriate behaviors are left unchecked. For example, studies show that children with untreated ADHD experience greater peer rejection, have higher injury rates, and experience higher rates of substance abuse and antisocial behavior. Their families experience high rates of marital discord, parental frustration, and divorce (Bloomquist, 1996).

We think that the whole question of whether or not to use medications is more easily answered when considering the following question: Do the benefits outweigh any potential risks or annoying side effects?

Common Medications to Treat ADHD

Although there are a number of potentially useful medications for treating ADHD, the vast majority of children are prescribed a stimulant medication to try first. Stimulant medications are typically the first choice primarily because this class of medications has been available for many years and stimulants have a long, relatively safe track record when used appropriately. There are few potentially serious side effects associated with these medicines, and they are relatively easy to administer and are available in a wide variety of brand names and *delivery systems*. Stimulants have consistently been demonstrated to improve attention, hyperactivity, and impulsivity significantly better than placebos in numerous studies. (Well over 300 studies involving stimulant usage in children with ADHD have been published.) While there are numerous stimulants currently on the market in the United States, most can be subcategorized into either the *methylphenidate-based* stimulant products (e.g., Ritalin, Concerta, Metadate, Focalin, and Daytrana) or the *methamphetamine-based* stimulant products (e.g., Dexedrine, Adderall, and Vyvanse). Within each stimulant class, products differ primarily in how rapidly they take effect and how long they continue to exert their behavioral and cognitive effects.

Generally, about 75% of all children with ADHD will respond well to a methylphenidate stimulant, and for those who don't seem to get an optimal response or who don't seem to tolerate methylphenidate products, about 75% of these children will then respond well to a methamphetamine product. The converse is also true if a methamphetamine product is the first medication tried. (Although in my personal clinical experience with many thousands of patients with ADHD, methylphenidate products tend to be slightly less potent or robust than methamphetamine products because of a difference in the way they work in the brain, but methylphenidate products are better tolerated by a larger proportion of patients.)

A review of Table 6.1 reveals that most stimulants begin to take effect within the first hour of administration. There are several older *short-acting* stimulant preparations that actively exert their effects for three to four hours. In the past several years, a great deal of research has been done to

Table 6.1 Stimulant Medications for ADHD

Stimulant Generic Name	Stimulant Trade Name	Typical Dosage Range in mg/Dose	Onset of Behavioral Effect in Minutes	Approximate Duration of Action in Hours
Methylphenidate	Ritalin	5–20	20–30	3–4
Methylphenidate (sustained-release)	Ritalin SR	10–40	45–60	6–8
Methylphenidate (extended-release)	Metadate ER	10–40	45–60	6–8
Methylphenidate (immediate + extended-release)	Metadate CD	10–40	20–30	6–8
Methylphenidate (long-acting)	Ritalin LA	10–40	20–30	6–8
Methylphenidate (extended-release)	Concerta	18–72	20–30	11–12
Methylphenidate adhesive patch	Daytrana	10–30	60–120	10–12
Dexmethylphenidate	Focalin	2.5–10	20–30	3–4
Dexmethylphenidate (extended-release)	Focalin XR	5–20	20–30	6–8
Dextroamphetamine	Dexedrine	2.5–10	20–30	3–4
Dextroamphetamine (sustained-release)	Dexedrine Spansules	5–20	45–60	6–8
Mixed amphetamine salts	Adderall	5–20	20–30	5–6
Mixed amphetamine salts	Adderall XR	10–40	20–30	10–12
Lisdexamfetamine	Vyvanse	20–70	30–60	11–13
Modafinil (not FDA approved for ADHD)	Provigil/ Sparlon	340–425	60–120	10–14

develop progressively longer-acting stimulant medications to effectively treat symptoms continuously throughout the entire school day. Medications such as Concerta, Adderall XR, Vyvanse, and Daytrana (a methylphenidate patch designed to be placed on the child's hip in the morning and removed daily after nine hours) can provide symptom relief for 10 to 12 hours daily and give children the ability to maintain their concentration and attention on late afternoon or early evening projects or homework, with the convenience and improvement in medication compliance offered by once daily medication.

Although the methylphenidate and methamphetamine products have traditionally been, and continue to be, prescribed as the *first-line* treatment of ADHD in children, several other medications can be used, particularly when stimulants are not tolerated or are not completely effective by themselves.

Atomoxetine (Strattera) was approved by the FDA in November of 2002 for the treatment of ADHD in children, adolescents, and adults. Strattera is a nonstimulant medication with stimulant-like properties. It is often used in children who fail to tolerate or fail to respond to traditional stimulants. At low doses, which are less stimulating but often less effective for treating core ADHD symptoms than higher doses, Strattera may have a calming effect and often helps children who have high levels of anxiety along with their ADHD. For children who benefit from, but don't tolerate sufficient doses of stimulants to get a full response, adding low dose Strattera to the stimulant is a strategy employed by an increasing number of physicians. Parents and teachers need to be aware that unlike the stimulants that deliver an immediate response once the *optimal* dose is found, Strattera may need to be given daily for up to two months in children before its effectiveness can be fully ascertained, and most doctors feel that response rates overall to Strattera tend to be much lower than response rates to stimulants.

Wellbutrin (bupropion) is an antidepressant with stimulant properties that is frequently used in adolescents and less frequently used in children, as there are very limited studies assessing Wellbutrin in the pediatric population. It is most typically used by doctors to treat ADHD when depression is also present, but it has been shown to have some efficacy in the treatment of nondepressed children with ADHD (Conners, Casat, Gualtieri, & Weller, 1996). Response rates to Wellbutrin tend to be low compared with response rates to stimulants, but stimulants in low doses can be safely combined with conservative doses of Wellbutrin if needed.

The *alpha-agonists* Catapress (clonidine) and Tenex (guanfacine) are nonstimulants (traditionally used as blood pressure medications at high doses) and are most commonly used in combination with stimulants to control hyperactivity, impulsivity, aggression, insomnia, tics, and oppositional-defiant symptoms when these problems are associated with ADHD (Arnsten, Steere, & Hunt, 1996; Chappell et al., 1995; Hunt, Armsten, & Asbell, 1995; Scahill et al., 2001). They can be sedating but very helpful.

The tricyclic antidepressants (e.g., Imipramine, Desipramine, Nortriptyline) are an older class of nonstimulant medications that have been shown to be effective for ADHD in children but are not commonly used because they tend to be less effective than stimulants and often have annoying side effects (like sedation, dry mouth, constipation, and, rarely, cardiac problems) that limit their use. They are most commonly used in those unusual circumstances where stimulants are having a tendency to cause or exacerbate underlying motor tics or when enuresis (urinary incontinence) is a problem along with a child's ADHD symptoms.

Until recently, if a low-dose stimulant was effective at treating symptoms of inattention only, then it had been the preferred practice to simply raise the dosage higher and higher in a sometimes futile attempt to effectively target impulsivity and hyperactivity. This approach does work for some children, but in many cases, this just leads to the emergence of more side effects from the medicine with little further improvement in symptoms. Despite concerns about using more than one medication at a time, many practitioners have found that two medications used together at low doses may yield a dramatically greater response and treat more of the child's symptoms with fewer associated side effects than using a high-dose stimulant alone.

There are many additional adjunctive medications currently available to treat symptoms or disorders that coexist with ADHD. Please discuss the possible benefits and risks of these medications with your prescribing physician.

CHANGES IN STUDENTS ON STIMULANTS

Although stimulants appear to have some potential to help with the full range of *core* ADHD symptoms, their greatest strength tends to lie with their ability to improve one's capacity to maintain focus and to stay on task. Studies have also noted overall improvement with stimulants in social situations in that the medication tends to reduce the intensity and improve the quality of peer interactions. Impulse control, fine motor coordination, restlessness, reaction time, and even short-term memory have been shown to improve as well. Aggressive behavior is often reduced with stimulants, but frequently, the addition of secondary medications and additional behavior management techniques are necessary to control problematic aggressive behavior or severe emotional outbursts.

Do Stimulants Cure ADHD? How Do These Medicines Work?

Unfortunately, no known medication actually cures ADHD. Medicines may, however, help to control many of the symptoms and behaviors associated with ADHD. Stimulant medications fundamentally work by increasing levels of the neurotransmitters norepinephrine and dopamine in areas of the brain that are relatively underactive in those with ADHD (thereby *stimulating* these areas). Underactive structures that are involved in moderating motor activity and distractibility become more *aroused* (see Chapter 1, "What Causes ADHD?" for a more detailed discussion).

How Long Does It Take for the Medication to Work?

As noted earlier, most stimulants exert their effects within the first hour of administration and are in the system for the next 3 to 12 hours, depending on the specific stimulant given. Consequently, on a given dosage, one should theoretically know if the medicine is effective shortly after the first dose. These medicines don't generally need repeated administration of a specific dose for one to know if they are going to be helpful. In reality, however, it isn't always easy to assess effectiveness after one dose, and it may take a few days to know for certain just how helpful a particular dose of medicine is. Perhaps the most common reason for uncertainty is that there are any number of daily events or stresses in a child's life that potentially influence behavior. If, for example, children are upset because they have just been grounded by their parents for failing to do their household chores for the past six days in a row, then it is unlikely that they will suddenly be cooperative and focused on their schoolwork the day they get their first dose of Ritalin. In other words, a pattern of responsiveness or failure to respond to a particular dose of a new medication is necessary to rule out the possibility of just having an unusually good or bad day when assessing medication effectiveness. If uncertain, it's important to communicate with the parents and/or doctor about any questions you may have regarding children's behavior.

Signs of Being Overmedicated

Enough medicine is when you see significant improvement in the ADHD symptoms without significant side effects. The most common signs indicating that too much medicine is being given are as follows.

1. Children look wired. They are more hyperactive and seem jittery or shaky and are more anxious and uncomfortable. All the ADHD symptoms seem worse.

2. The children look lethargic, look zombie-like, or look as though they are withdrawn and without any of their usual spunk. If children look lethargic, you should communicate this observation to the parents and doctor.

IF THE MEDICINE WORKS, DOES THAT CONFIRM THAT THE DIAGNOSIS OF ADHD IS CORRECT?

Not necessarily. Stimulants, including caffeine, tend to improve attention in most people at some dosage. For example, if a sufficient dose of Ritalin was given to 100 children or adults, we would likely note measurable improvement in attention and in freedom from distractibility in the majority of these individuals. Those few who don't respond are usually either (a) individuals who are unusually sensitive to annoying or adverse side effects to stimulants or (b) those that have coexisting problems with their ADHD such as severe anxiety, depression, or bipolar disorder. The crucial point here is that in those individuals identified as having the greatest problem with attention (i.e., those with ADHD), we would likely see very dramatic prestimulant versus poststimulant differences in these individuals' ability to attend to a particular task. Those individuals with no notable problem focusing in the first place, however, would likely only see minor improvements in their ability to focus after taking the Ritalin. In summary, although a positive response to stimulants won't diagnose ADHD, in most cases, those who do have ADHD will respond significantly.

SIDE EFFECTS FROM STIMULANTS

Although the extreme abuse of stimulants in adults has been known to cause central nervous system damage, vascular damage, and hypertension, virtually none of these problems occur with the standard dosages used to treat ADHD symptoms. The vast majority of healthy children prescribed routine doses of stimulants have either no significant side effects or mild tolerable side effects. Most side effects are dose related, so the higher the dose used the greater the likelihood that some annoying side effect will emerge. At routine doses, it is extraordinarily rare to see any medically dangerous side effects in a healthy child.

Appetite Suppression

The most common side effect from stimulants in children that I encounter is appetite suppression. In most cases, this side effect is easily managed by simply administering the stimulant with or following meals. Sometimes, switching a child to an alternate stimulant will cause less appetite suppression. Another alternative is to do nothing and see if the appetite suppression, if mild, will simply resolve in a few weeks on its own with continued use of the stimulant, as frequently is the case. If all else fails, doctors can add a medicine such as an antihistamine to stimulate appetite, but this is almost never necessary. Feeding children high calorie, healthy foods before the stimulant takes effect and after the stimulant wears off is usually sufficient.

Insomnia

Another common but easily managed side effect is insomnia. As most of us who use caffeine know, taking a stimulant too close to bedtime can cause insomnia. Simply adjusting the timing of the dosing so that the stimulant is out of the system by bedtime will solve the problem in most cases. For children whose ADHD itself is the primary reason they have trouble falling asleep, sometimes an evening dose of a stimulant actually allows for improvement in the insomnia by decreasing the hyperactive behavior and the difficulty *gearing down* for bed that is so often seen in these children. If all else fails, low doses of other medications such as Benadryl (diphenhydramine) or Catapress (clonidine) given at bedtime can be used to help a child get to sleep whether the stimulant is contributing to the problem or not. There are also a wide variety of over-the-counter herbal teas and preparations that can help with this problem.

Mild Headaches or Stomach Upset

Mild headaches or stomach upset are occasionally noted with a particular stimulant. Usually, these two side effects rapidly resolve on their own with continued use of the stimulant, but if not, a dosage decrease or a change in the kind of stimulant used or even a change in the drug manufacturer (if generic stimulants are prescribed) will most often help.

Motor Tics

Motor tics are sudden involuntary muscle contractions that can involve virtually any muscle in the body. Stimulant medications are often blamed for causing or exacerbating them, but this has been difficult to confirm as motor tics typically wax and wane with or without stimulants. Most experts now believe that roughly equal percentages of affected children experience exacerbation, improvement, and no change with stimulant medications. When a teacher or counselor observes a tic, the parent should be notified so the child's doctor can assess this observation.

Rebound Effect

The *rebound effect* is another common but generally manageable phenomenon that can occur when stimulant medications rapidly wear off. It is characterized by irritability and an exacerbation of those baseline ADHD symptoms that are noted without medication, such as impulsivity and hyperactivity. Sometimes the child's mood is depressed, but in any event, it is an unpleasant experience if your student has this each time the stimulant wears off. Fortunately, these symptoms, when present, will tend to only last for 30 to 60 minutes followed by a return to the child's baseline.

With the widespread use of longer acting stimulants, rebound effect is much less common than it used to be when only shorter acting stimulants were available. The long-acting preparations tend to leave the system more slowly and, hence, have a lower likelihood of causing this problem. One can also try overlapping dosages by always giving the second stimulant dose (when using a short-acting stimulant) at least 20 to 30 minutes *before* the rebound effect occurs from the first dose wearing off. Because rebound effects are dose related, if the second stimulant dosage is lower than the first dose, the risk of rebound when the second dose wears off will be reduced.

Common Side Effects of Strattera

The most common side effects noted with Strattera (atomoxetine) are abdominal discomfort, nausea, decreased appetite, irritability, and drowsiness. Most of these side effects are transient and manageable if the child's dosage is increased very slowly over several weeks.

INFORMATION THAT SHOULD BE COMMUNICATED TO THE DOCTOR

Good communication between the school counselor and the doctor is extremely valuable, particularly when starting or adjusting medications. Unfortunately, many physicians have practices that severely limit their ability to communicate on the phone, so counselors are often left feeling that their input is not valued. On the contrary, teachers and school counselors have the unique experience of being able to observe large numbers of children of a particular age group, so they may be the first observer to notice when a particular child is functioning outside the norm. This knowledge and information is critical for the physician in his or her assessment of the child. Ongoing observations by the teacher and school counselor are also essential when deciding whether or not a medication is being administered at the optimal dosage, especially if a shorter acting stimulant is being used for school only. If this is the case, the teacher and school counselor may be the only adults who have direct knowledge of the response to the medication or of any problematic side effects, such as excessive sedation or agitation. Once the parents sign the appropriate consent form, your observations can be communicated by fax, e-mail, or phone to the physician's ancillary staff (physician assistant, nurse, or nurse practitioner) if the doctor is unavailable.

CAN STIMULANTS CAUSE PROBLEMS WITH GROWTH?

Generally speaking, the answer is no. For many years, there has been speculation that stimulants can cause growth deficits in children, and some early studies seemed to lend support to this idea. However, more recent studies seem to indicate that growth deficits are extremely rare, and if they occur at all, they are not likely to result in more than one half inch to one inch of growth inhibition over the child's life span. Instead, studies suggest that small but significant differences in height previously attributed to stimulants are in fact associated statistically with having an ADHD diagnosis and are less likely to be related to the treatment of ADHD. Some children with ADHD appear to experience their most significant adolescent growth spurt at slightly later ages than in their nonaffected peer group, but they tend to catch up to their peer group by late adolescence (Biederman et al., 2003; Biederman, Spencer, & Faraone, 2003; Spencer, 2003; Spencer et al., 1996).

ARE STIMULANTS ADDICTIVE?

Although prescription stimulants like Ritalin, Dexedrine, and Adderall all carry strong warnings regarding their *addictive potential*, in practice, actual drug addiction (or *drug dependence*, as is now the preferred and more precise term) is quite rare when these medications are used as prescribed. Two of the most important components of drug dependence are (a) tolerance and (b) withdrawal. Tolerance refers to either a need to take progressively higher doses of a medication to achieve the desired effect, or it refers to a diminished effect with continued use of the same amount of the substance. As most of us are aware, drugs such as nicotine, alcohol, Valium, and even the stimulant caffeine are associated with the development of significant tolerance. Most readers of this book who drink several cups of coffee daily can readily attest to this phenomenon from their personal experience. When heavy coffee consumers abruptly quit drinking coffee, they are well aware of the severe fatigue and withdrawal headaches that often occur. These drugs also have significant withdrawal syndromes associated with their abrupt discontinuation.

With respect to the issue of tolerance, prescription stimulants prescribed for ADHD in standard dosages rarely result in the development of tolerance. (Caffeine is the notable exception among the stimulants, and it is not a particularly good drug for treating ADHD.) If tolerance does develop, discontinuing the medication for several days and then restarting at the previous dosage or changing to a different stimulant (as there is rarely any significant *cross-tolerance* from one stimulant to the next) can resolve the issue. Thus, the stimulants do not need to be used on a daily basis to be effective and can be discontinued abruptly at any time if desired without any adverse medical consequences. Obviously, the underlying ADHD symptoms will rapidly return with medication discontinuation, as stimulants will not cure ADHD but will merely treat symptoms of ADHD while the medication is in the bloodstream. It should also be noted that we occasionally see individuals for whom abrupt discontinuation of the stimulant after prolonged daily use will result in a day or two of feeling drowsy in addition to the return of their underlying ADHD symptoms.

CAN STIMULANTS LEAD TO PROBLEMS WITH ABUSE OF OTHER DRUGS?

Children with untreated ADHD are already at higher-than-average risk for substance abuse for several possible reasons. Poor impulse control, low self-esteem, defiant behavior, and impairment of social skills are all commonly seen in children with ADHD, and any of these factors would tend to increase one's eventual risk of experimenting with or abusing illicit drugs as a teenager or adult.

Consequently, there would be justifiable concern if such risks were to somehow be further increased by the treatment of ADHD with *powerful stimulant drugs.* Many teachers and parents worry that giving children a pill might give them the message that pills are an easy way to solve life's problems or that the *addictiveness of stimulants* might multiply the risk of abusing other drugs.

Current studies on this issue actually suggest that stimulant use for treatment of ADHD does *not* lead to later abuse of other drugs. There is, in fact, evidence to suggest that aggressive treatment of ADHD may actually *decrease* the likelihood of abusing other drugs, perhaps because aggressive treatment over time may directly or indirectly reduce many of the factors noted earlier that put children with ADHD at risk in the first place.

This is not to say that the use of stimulants is risk free. Treatment with stimulants needs to be considered only with great caution, for instance, in teens who are already identified to be abusing other drugs. When substance abuse is an issue but ADHD needs to be treated, Strattera, Vyvanse, Wellbutrin, and Concerta (methylphenidate in a delivery system with low abuse potential) are all reasonable options and alternatives to the traditional stimulants. With respect to the relevant concern that giving a pill to a child sends a negative message, it is always important to teach children the difference between taking a pill to treat a legitimate medical problem versus the indiscriminate use and abuse of mood-altering drugs to either *get high* or to escape reality.

ARE THERE PARTICULAR CHILDREN WHO WOULD BE EXPECTED TO DO POORLY ON STIMULANTS?

Although there are few absolute contraindications to the use of stimulants, there are certain groups for whom stimulants are generally either not recommended or for whom they should be used with greater caution. The first of these would include those with psychotic disorders, such as schizophrenia, in whom stimulants have the potential to exacerbate psychotic symptoms, such as paranoia or auditory hallucinations. The routine use of stimulants would not normally be expected to cause any of these symptoms in children with a diagnosis of ADHD alone but might do so in psychotic children with schizophrenia or bipolar disorder, if their inattentiveness is mistaken for ADHD.

Similarly, any child with severe anxiety would be at risk for an exacerbation of their anxiety with the use of a stimulant medication. This group would include either those children who seem biologically predisposed to having high levels of anxiety or those children who are highly anxious or worried because of situational circumstances. An example might be the child who lives in a chaotic family environment or one who has been traumatized emotionally by significant abuse or neglect.

In the case of the anxious child with ADHD, the stimulant has the potential to help with the ADHD, but the stimulant will also have the potential to worsen ADHD symptoms by exacerbating the anxiety. Likewise for depressed children with underlying ADHD, stimulants may at times appear mildly helpful, but if the depressive disorder is significant, then the child's ADHD symptoms will not likely improve to any meaningful degree until the depression is adequately treated.

Other situations where stimulants are not consistently helpful might include their use in the treatment of children who appear to have ADHD-like symptoms associated with intrauterine drug exposure, traumatic brain injuries, or pervasive developmental disorders such as autism. These are not hard and fast rules as some children in these groups may respond positively to stimulants, but children in these categories appear to be at higher-than-average risk for a worsening of their behavioral problems with the use of stimulants.

Stimulants also are not likely to directly improve learning disabilities or oppositional-defiant disorders, but they may help if ADHD is clearly present, underlying, or alongside these problems. The use of stimulants in children with substance abuse problems is another category where there is a relative contraindication as was discussed earlier.

ARE THERE CHILDREN WHO ONLY NEED TO BE ON MEDICATION AT SCHOOL?

Although there is perhaps no correct answer to this question, my own philosophy is to recommend stimulant medication every day for those children with ADHD whose impulsivity or hyperactivity lead to emotional outbursts or behavioral problems that improve whenever the stimulant is taken. In these children, withholding medication on weekends doesn't make sense if the inevitable outcome is eruption into chaos. Increasingly, I am recommending medication daily for the majority of children with ADHD that I treat (even in those without serious behavior problems) because so many of them have multiple deficits that tend to improve with medication and because there are so few problems associated with taking the medication daily. (As noted earlier, tolerance, appetite suppression, and insomnia from the medication are rarely significant problems.)

On the other hand, there are some children with ADHD who have no unusual social or behavioral problems and are primarily taking the stimulant to improve attention in the classroom or to complete homework after school. In these individuals, unless there is some unusual activity to complete on a weekend or holiday that requires a great deal of attention, it is not *mandatory* for these children to take their stimulants on weekends or holidays, especially because there is typically no identified set of symptoms associated with abrupt discontinuation of stimulants (i.e., a *withdrawal syndrome*).

DRUG INTERACTIONS WITH STIMULANT MEDICATION

There are very few problematic drug interactions with stimulants, but there may be times, as a school counselor, that you observe children who appear to vary in their response to a stable dose of medication on different days without any apparent environmental or *untreated mood component* on top of their ADHD to explain the problem.

One possible, and infrequently recognized, cause might be the combination of the stimulant taken with a breakfast containing *organic acids* such as ascorbic acid (vitamin C) or citric acid (in orange or cranberry juice). Other possible culprits include oral suspension antibiotics, Pop-Tarts, power bars, granola bars, and Gatorade. All of these substances, which can create an acidic stomach environment, can interfere with proper absorption of the medication and are best avoided for at least 30 to 45 minutes before or after taking the medication if a consistent response to a particular dose of a stimulant is desired. The methylphenidate-based, long-acting medications Concerta (taken orally) and Daytrana (the methylphenidate patch) appear to be largely unaffected by these issues because of their unique delivery systems (Auiler, Liu, Lynch, & Gelotte, 2002; Modi, Wang, Hu, & Gupta, 2000). Once the medication begins to take effect, these acidic substances are no longer a problem. Grapefruit juice, however, presents its own unique problem in that it contains enzymes that may cause dramatic *increases* in absorption of a variety of medications. Consequently, I recommend avoiding grapefruit juice entirely to anyone taking medication unless a pharmacist is able to verify that there is no interaction with the specific medication being taken.

It is important that you share with the parents any behaviors that seem unusual or raise questions in your mind. The parents should be encouraged to share your thoughts with the child's doctor.

CAN CHILDREN BECOME PSYCHOTIC ON STIMULANTS?

Stimulants used *appropriately* in the absence of any disorder associated with psychotic symptoms (e.g., schizophrenia or bipolar disorder) will *not* normally cause psychotic symptoms. (I have only seen one case in my 20 years of prescribing stimulants.) In rare cases, it may be possible to induce temporary psychotic symptoms in susceptible individuals by administering stimulants far in excess of their recommended dosages. Prolonged abuse of stimulants at many times their recommended dosage may eventually lead to a *schizophrenic-like* presentation, but this is simply not an issue with judicious use of prescription stimulants.

CAN STIMULANTS BE USED IN CHILDREN UNDER AGE FIVE?

Yes, but with several caveats. First, stimulant use is not well studied in children this young, and there are theoretical concerns about exposing very young children to stimulants (especially children less than four years of age) when so little is known about how these medications may affect very early brain development, although no unique medical problems have been identified in children under age five that would absolutely contraindicate stimulant usage. Perhaps an equally important reason to withhold prescribing in children this young is that it is difficult to be certain in this age group whether the ADHD diagnosis is accurate, even though the majority of children who later turn out to actually have diagnosable ADHD in grade school do historically manifest symptoms of ADHD prior to first grade. In such young children, it can be difficult to fully evaluate other problems that can mimic ADHD (e.g., developmental disabilities or simple immaturity). Additionally, most of the psychological tests used in an educational setting to assess for the presence of learning disabilities are simply not available for use in such young children (Firestone, Musten, Pisterman, Mercer, & Bennett, 1998; Minde, 1998; Rappley et al., 1999; Short, Manos, Findling, & Schubel, 2004; Zito et al., 2000).

Another complicating variable is that commercially available doses of many stimulants may be too potent for such small children, and it can be difficult to divide some stimulants preparations into small enough fractions of a pill to be practical. (This is becoming less of a problem over time with so many different stimulant products now available.) Longer acting stimulant preparations are preferred in young children because this population tends to metabolize the short-acting stimulant preparations very rapidly, necessitating frequent dosing throughout the day (which is often impractical). Frequent dosing of short-acting stimulants can lead to potentially significant rebound effects. The largest study to date examining this issue found that stimulants could be effectively used but that these children experienced slower growth rates than their peers and experienced more irritability, insomnia, and appetite suppression than in older children on stimulants (Greenhill et al., 2006). Under these circumstances the child, parent, teacher, and school counselor may feel like the child is on a mood roller coaster.

My advice is to try to wait until grade school, if possible, before placing a child on medication.

MY STUDENT USED TO DO WELL ON RITALIN, BUT NOW IT DOESN'T WORK. WHAT IS GOING ON?

If the issue is an on-again-off-again response to stimulants where the medicine seems to work well at times and then not to work at all, then the possibility of an underlying mood disorder is suggested. Mood disorders usually interfere with one's ability to attend and to concentrate so that one's ADHD symptoms will appear to be at their worst when mood symptoms are prominent. If ADHD symptoms tend to disappear completely when one's mood is normal while other home and school variables are unchanged, then the actual diagnosis of ADHD becomes doubtful. If ADHD symptoms are merely a bit less pronounced than usual when one's mood is stable, then ADHD *and* a mood disorder are likely to both be present.

If the issue is not an on-again-off-again problem but rather is simply that the medication no longer is as helpful as it used to be, then a slight dose increase may be indicated. It is possible that because of the child's growth the medication is simply no longer effective at its current dosage. Another possibility is that some tolerance to the medication has developed over time. If tolerance seems to be the issue, it is worth asking the parents to speak with the doctor about a *drug holiday* to assess for this possibility. Unfortunately, temporary discontinuation of the medication may not always be practical if the child's behavior is unmanageable without the medication, in which case it may be necessary to switch to a different class of medication.

NATURAL REMEDIES TO TREAT ADHD

The term *natural remedies* generally refers to those substances used for medicinal purposes that are found in relatively unaltered states in the environment—as opposed to the *unnatural* pharmaceutical drugs that are synthesized in laboratories. Natural remedies are popularly thought of as safe, and synthetic unnatural drugs are often considered by the lay public to be potentially hazardous. The problem with what seems to be a simple distinction, however, is that natural remedies are not always safe or adequately tested, and many are processed in unnatural ways before they reach the consumer. Furthermore, many pharmaceutical drugs are actually derived from natural sources, and some that are entirely synthetic may be quite safe or may be chemically indistinguishable from similar substances of natural origin. In other words, the boundaries between natural and unnatural remedies are fuzzy at best.

Having said this, there may be a place for the use of certain supplements to *augment* the response to stimulants in some children with ADHD (as opposed to using these remedies as *alternatives* to stimulants). For example, ADHD has been found to be associated with a deficiency of essential fatty acids in some children (Colquhoun & Bunday, 1981; Stevens et al., 1995) and that supplementing the diet with essential fatty acids, usually given in the form of fish oil, may reduce ADHD symptoms

(Burgess, 1998; Richardson & Ross, 2000). Essential fatty acids, particularly the omega-3 fatty acid known as DHA, play a critical role in the brain and central nervous system throughout the life span and are "essential for normal neuronal structure and function, maintenance of membrane fluidity, impulse transmission, receptor sensitivity, and maintenance of adequate neurotransmitter pool" (Horrobin, Glen, & Hudson, 1995, p. 605). Although studies in this area are very promising, it should be emphasized that ADHD symptoms did not disappear entirely with fish oil alone and that the positive results in one study were seen primarily in children who manifested clinical signs consistent with a deficiency of essential fatty acids (e.g., frequent urination, excessive thirst, dry skin, and dry hair) (Mitchell, Aman, Turbott, & Manku, 1987).

With respect to specific vitamins or minerals, several small studies have found levels of zinc, iron, B vitamins, and magnesium to be lower in children with ADHD than in control groups (Kozielec & Starobrat-Hermelin, 1997; Toren et al., 1996). It is possible that restoring deficient levels to normal could improve ADHD symptoms in some individuals. Although there are no studies to validate the use of megavitamin doses, smaller doses of certain specific vitamins or minerals may be helpful. For example, one study, where 150 milligrams of zinc were added to stimulant treatment, noted significant improvement in impulsive behaviors and socialization skills compared with the placebo (Arnold et al., 2005). Another study demonstrated improvement in ADHD symptoms with one month of iron supplementation (Konofal, Cortese, Lecendreux, Arnulf, & Mouren, 2005). Significant behavioral improvement was noted in a majority of children with ADHD when daily vitamin B6 was administered with 100 milligrams of magnesium (Mousain-Bosc et al., 2006).

With respect to herbal supplements, some small studies have been notable. Panax quinquefolius (200 mg) along with gingko biloba (50 mg) given twice daily for one month demonstrated improvement in ADHD in a majority of 36 children with ADHD (Lyon et al., 2001), and L-theonine (an amino acid found in green tea) has been found to improve ADHD symptoms and to decrease anxiety.

In response to observations that some children show hyperactive behavior associated with certain foods (especially sugar), food dyes, chocolate, and other additives, various *elimination* diets have been tried. The best known of these is the Feingold diet. Several double-blind placebo-controlled studies have failed to support the Feingold diet or the dietary effects of sugar on behavior (Egger, Stella, & McEwen, 1992; Wolraich, Wilson & White, 1995). A great deal of media attention was given to a study in 2007 (McCann et al., 2007) that seemed to suggest that ADHD could be caused by some common food additives found in junk food.

In this study, children from the general population in the United Kingdom were given a drink laden with food dyes and a common preservative (sodium benzoate). The study was notable in that a significant percentage of the children (a group of three-year-olds and another group of eight- and nine-year-olds) demonstrated an increase in hyperactive symptoms that "lend strong support for the case that food additives exacerbate hyperactive behaviors (inattention, impulsivity, and overactivity) in children at least up to middle childhood" (McCann et al., 2007, p. 1556). Few would argue about the importance and the validity of this study, and hopefully, it will lead to further studies on the possible adverse effects of a wide variety of food additives (many of which, especially in the case of food dyes, are of very questionable necessity). In my practice, I routinely refer to this study as a lesson to parents about the importance of a healthy diet. Nonetheless, what seems to have been missed in the media coverage is that the degree to which the additives increased hyperactive symptoms was mild in most cases that it was observed. Food additives did exacerbate hyperactive behaviors, and the results did reach a convincing level of statistical significance but not to a sufficient degree to cause the full range and severity of symptoms associated with a diagnosis of ADHD.

The temptation to find a natural approach to treatment (as an *alternative* to medication) can be very strong. Most of us would like to use approaches to treatment that offer the greatest benefit with the fewest risks, but unfortunately, *natural* or *herbal* does not always mean *safer*. Additionally, many parents feel that they can somehow avoid the stigma associated with either the ADHD diagnosis or with the use of stimulants by using alternative therapies.

Unfortunately, even if these approaches do not end up being toxic, they may have adverse consequences for a child if they significantly delay the usage of more thoroughly researched medications where potential risks versus benefits are better known.

There is at least one important reason why natural treatments are often less well-studied than are more traditional medications. Because natural remedies are by definition found in nature, these substances cannot, generally speaking, be easily patented by companies wishing to package and promote their use. The patent system was designed to give a person or company exclusive rights to research, to develop, and to market a product for a predetermined period of time. Once a patent is obtained, a company no longer needs to worry (for several years) that their own research and development dollars will allow a competing second or third company to borrow and profit from that research by marketing the same product with minimal investment. Therefore, without the ability to patent an herbal remedy, there traditionally has been little incentive for private companies to spend money on research. However, because of dramatic recent increases in the general public's interest in herbal remedies in the United States, there is increasing movement by both private enterprise and the government to fund research in this area.

PROZAC AS A TREATMENT FOR ADHD

Prozac (fluoxetine) is in a class of medications known as the *SSRIs* (selective serotonin reuptake inhibitors). Other medications in this class are Zoloft (sertraline), Paxil (paroxetine), Luvox (fluvoxamine), Celexa (citalopram), and Lexapro (escitalopram). All are similar in their mechanism of action in the brain, yet all are slightly different from each other and none will directly target the core symptoms of ADHD. Despite that fact, they are frequently used in children with ADHD when significant symptoms or signs of anxiety, depression, or obsessive-compulsiveness are present. The medications in this class can be extremely helpful for improving hyperreactivity (as opposed to hyperactivity) in that when they are effective they tend to significantly improve a person's ability to take things in stride so that the person is less likely to become easily overwhelmed. This class of medication should be used cautiously; however, if bipolar disorder is suspected in the child, the use of antidepressants without first using mood stabilizers could exacerbate manic symptoms or mood cycling in these cases. These medications need to be taken daily for maximum effectiveness, and in some cases, missing doses can result in severe withdrawal, agitation, and dizziness.

DO MEDICATIONS HELP LEARNING DISABILITIES?

There really are no medications at this point in time that are known to directly improve learning disabilities (also known as developmental disorders). Nonetheless, if ADHD symptoms or other medication-responsive problems are present along with the learning disability, then at least the medication can effectively be used to target these areas. Once these associated treatable problems are better, the impairment from the disability itself can be more clearly seen and may appear to be less severe than originally thought.

ONE OF MY STUDENTS IS VERY DEFIANT AND OPPOSITIONAL. WILL MEDICATIONS HELP WITH THIS?

Not directly in most cases. ODD is frequently seen along with ADHD, especially in cases where the ADHD goes untreated for several years.

Children with this problem are often irritable and angry and tend to lose their tempers often. They regularly argue with their parents and teachers and tend to blame someone else whenever they get into trouble. They actively defy rules and, in more severe cases, may eventually end up in trouble with the law.

Occasionally, these symptoms are part of an underlying depressive disorder where the use of antidepressant medications will likely reduce the severity of these symptoms. More commonly, however, the ODD is not found to be associated with a depressive disorder, in which case the appropriate treatment is to address the ADHD with medication and to learn as many of the other behavioral-management strategies that you can from other sections in this book. Frequently, some direct improvement of ODD symptoms results from stimulant treatment alone. Often, improvement will come over time from the combination of stimulant treatment, appropriate behavioral management, and gradual improvement in self-esteem. Despite the absence of any universally acceptable medication for this problem, in desperation many parents and psychiatrists will try medications, such as antidepressants, alpha agonists (e.g., Catapress or Tenex), neuroleptic medications (e.g., Abilify, Zyprexa, Seroquel, Risperdal), or the anticonvulsants/mood stabilizers (e.g., Depakote, Lithium, Trileptal), in their attempt to mitigate the often associated symptoms of impulsivity or aggression. At times, these other medications can be quite helpful.

SUMMARY

The decision parents make to medicate their child can be a difficult one. It's therefore important for school counselors not only to show sympathy and understanding for parents' anxiety and concerns around medicating their child for ADHD, but also to understand the benefits and limitations of medication in the treatment of ADHD. This chapter's intent was to inform you about the usefulness as well as the limitations of using medication and has tried to answer some of the most common questions that parents and school counselors have about the actual use of specific medications for ADHD.

I discussed the various medications used to treat ADHD. I reviewed the most common side effects and complications associated with the use of stimulant medications and discussed the various options for managing problems that might arise in treatment.

7 Communicating Effectively With Parents

When parents of affected children meet with a school counselor for the first time, they often seem to be carrying a backpack loaded with bad experiences from contacts over their child with schools, relatives, spouses, and neighbors. The child's school, like a next-door neighbor, can be seen as one more additional stress to parents, sometimes triggering feelings of resentment and anger. Consequently, how the school communicates with the parents can make a significant difference in their attitudes, revealing either parents who want to work with the school or parents who want to stay away.

PARENTS: THE MOST IMPORTANT RESOURCE

By the time a child reaches school age, parents will have invested many hours caring, nurturing, and keeping safe their child. Raising a child is neither conflict free nor is it easy; however, for parents of affected children, it can be even more challenging. A child who presents, sometimes daily, behaviors that keep the soup boiling can and will trigger feelings of frustration. Some parents have expressed that just *to survive*, they find themselves talking with their child's doctor often, going to local and state conferences on ADHD, and paying out hard-earned money to see an ADHD specialist; and their home library becomes a self-help section on ADHD. In many ways, the parents become experts on this disorder as it relates to their child. So they should never be dismissed or ignored when it comes to helping the teacher understand their child's behavior. Parents can be a gold mine for ideas on best practices in working with their child. Unfortunately, if there is a breakdown in communication or trust between the school and parents, this knowledge is lost. The consequence, sadly, is that when trust is lost both parents and school staff can come to loggerheads over the child's behavior. When this seems to be happening, the counselor needs to see their role as doing his or her best to assure that the parents are listened to, the teacher is heard, and the child is not caught in between upset adults.

RESPECT AND ACKNOWLEDGE THE CHALLENGES PARENTS FACE

Schools need to convey compassion, understanding, respect, and interest in the needs of affected children and their parents. By partnering with the parents, schools can find better ways to deal with the child's challenges. Blame is not helpful, and it reinforces, in the parents mind, the school's lack of appreciation for their struggles and effort.

As suggested in our earlier chapters, raising a child with ADHD is not easy under the best of circumstances. One parent described her situation as being similar to that of a dog on a chain—she had some freedom of movement and choices, but the chain could be pulled at any time, whether she liked it or not. She saw herself as so closely connected to her child's life that she sometimes felt "choked by his problems." She felt her child was in control and could pull her chain at will. Desperate for relief, this mother would fantasize about running away from home, leaving the family in the father's care. She knew she never would, but the thought often crossed her mind. Parents of affected children often feel they are in the eye of a storm and there is no relief in sight. At these moments, parents need respite from their child and the school problems, what Rudolf Dreikers calls a "mental withdrawal-to-the-bathroom," to escape from angry neighbors and upset teachers (Dreikers, 1964; Lougy & Rosenthal, 2002).

The counselor can play an important role in helping school staff recognize parents' efforts and acknowledging that the parents can be as frustrated as the school. The authors have experienced that most parents like their child's school and respect the important role their child's teacher plays. The parents of affected children know their children can be challenging and want to help. They just want the school not to dismiss their efforts or blame their child when the child comes up short in meeting a behavior and academic goal.

HELPING PARENTS DISTINGUISH ENABLING FROM SUPPORTIVE DECISIONS

Parents of affected children can be enabling, just like all parents. It is important to help parents make the distinction between when they are being enabling and when they are being supportive.

Affected parents can come to a place where they make excuses for their child's behavior. This is not good and is not in the best interest of the child. ADHD is not a "get-out-of-jail-free" card. Affected children, whether on medication or not, need to be held accountable for their behavior. Society will not tolerate behaviors that interfere with the safety and well-being of others. All children need to be taught ways to limit negative interactions with others and find better ways to control their impulsiveness. According to John Taylor (1994), parents need to stand behind their child, not protectively in front of the child. Parents need to learn to not run interference between their child and others. The affected children need to deal directly with others regarding their behavior. They need to know that their parents care about how they behave, and when they begin to feel their parents don't care about how they behave, they lose "an important motivation for remaining socialized" (Lougy & Rosenthal, 2002; Taylor, 1994, 2001).

So why do we sometimes find parents of affected children seeming to make excuses for their child's behavior? We suggest that the reasons can be many, but one theme that the authors have seen is that the parents' sense that they are "losing their child," in the words of Russell Barkley (1995). Out of the continuing discord between children and parents, there seems to develop a distancing that can be very painful to the parents. They can become moody, agitated, and irritable toward the child and other family members. The parents' sense that they lost their bond with their child—the child who takes so much patience and understanding and can make them feel, at times, unloved. Unfortunately, parents, trying to compensate for their feelings of guilt, can become enabling at the detriment of the child.

The school counselor can play a very important role in helping parents deal with these feelings or refer parents to outside counseling so the parents can begin to deal with their conflicting feelings toward their child. When parents feel less guilt and more secure in their relationship with their child, they are more amenable to educators' suggestions and are more likely to not run interference for their child.

Regular Communication Is Critical

Regular communication between the parents, teacher, and child is critical in maintaining continuity of treatment with an affected child. As mentioned in earlier chapters, affected children respond best to a multimodel treatment program. In working with affected children, the counselor needs to be proactive in assuring that all parties are communicating and the child's educational and social and emotional needs are maintained. The counselor's unique role provides the teacher, child, and parents the opportunity to express concerns and questions when important.

Once an intervention plan is established, the counselor should understand that they will need to be in continuing contact with the teacher, parents, and child on a regular basis. Preferably, the counselor should touch base with the teacher, child, or parents once a week until the child is doing better, and bimonthly communication with the teacher should be expected from then on. The authors have found that e-mails can help to touch base or answer questions. However, confidentiality concerns must always be discussed with the parent or teacher when using e-mails.

Often the parents will need support when asked to make changes at home around discipline procedures when the child gets in trouble at school. Parents can be very sensitive to perceived feelings of criticism or victimization, so the counselor needs to attend to these feelings when they are observed. However, if the relationship is trusting, the counselor generally can help the parents deal with changes that can feel very uncomfortable to them at first.

Teachers also can find change uncomfortable. Like parents, they sometimes will feel that too much is being asked of them or they are not totally comfortable with the interventions. The authors have found that providing teachers with information on ADHD to help them better understand the reasoning behind the changes can help. However, change is not easy and sometimes it is resisted by teachers or misguided administrators. When teachers or administration seem resistant or rigid to any change, it is often best to communicate that children with ADHD have civil rights protections, and it's advisable that the school set up a schoolwide plan to deal with these special children.

Attending Teacher-Parent Meetings

The school counselor is asked regularly to attend teacher-parent meetings when dealing with affected children. In fact, to not be invited would be of concern in that an important staff member is not participating or providing important input on the child's behalf. The school should see the school counselor as the one person who has the credentials and training to assess the child's progress and provide confidential communication with all parties involved. Consequently, a counselors needs to make it their priority to be at as many meetings as possible between the parent and teacher.

Counselors should see their role, as discussed earlier, as a consultant and not as an expert on ADHD. Counselors can reinforce and model the collaborative model in addressing the child's challenges. Often less emotionally involved or invested, counselors can bring to the meeting a unique and more detached perspective. The counselor can also assure that the child's point of view is shared, even if the child is too young to participate. Even older children can be intimidated by such meetings, and the counselor can be the child's voice.

It's important that the counselor be prepared to advocate for the child's civil rights when needed. Sometimes legal or civil rights issues are not recognized or are lost when the child's behaviors are severe. The counselor can bring to the meeting information to help assure that the child's civil rights are not ignored. The counselor can provide important input and guidance when reviewing and setting up interventions that address the child's disability.

Summary

We have emphasized throughout this book that children with ADHD are challenged in school and that, even with medication, some problem behaviors can only be tempered, not eliminated. Consequently, schools are always challenged finding ways to work with affected children.

Even under the best of educational environments, affected children can find themselves getting into trouble and being sent home. The dilemma for many children is that schools are often not ready for them and they are not ready for school. Options are generally limited for affected children when it comes to classroom accommodations. Schools, we suggest, are generally not providing the educational setting needed for these children to be more successful. Schools, generally, have been slow in implementing accommodations.

Even though schools cannot prevent the underlying neurological impairment found in children with ADHD or "fix" bad parenting, they can do a better job preventing these impairments from causing academic and social failure (Lougy & Rosenthal, 2002).

Hopefully we have given the reader new ideas, hope, and the knowledge and confidence to be open to fresh approaches to deal with these children. As suggested in our Preface, "As an educator, you must have an open mind, a flexible attitude, a willingness to go with the flow or change directions when needed, and, frankly, be adventurous and often realize that interventions are often guided by trial and error."

Good luck!

Resource A

Useful Web Sites for Parents and Teachers

Abilitations

http://www.abilitations.com

Abilitations is a company whose primary focus is serving the needs of individuals with special needs.

ADDitude

http://www.additude.com

ADDitude is a consumer-focused Web site designed to provide resources for children and adults with ADHD and learning disabilities. Resources include online information about the disorder, expert answers, tools (including a service directory), book reviews, Podcasts, blogs, news, and more.

Alpha Smart

http://www.alphasmart.com

Alpha Smart is a keyboarding device that supports the needs of students who struggle with written work. The keyboard provides students a chance to produce work electronically without the expense of a computer or laptop. All work done on the Alpha Smart can be downloaded wirelessly to a classroom computer for printing or editing.

All Kinds of Minds

http://www.allkindsofminds.org

The All Kinds of Minds Web site offers an online newsletter to support learning disabilities. This site is a great resource for information on characteristics of students with learning disabilities.

American Academy of Child and Adolescent Psychiatry (AACAP)

http://www.aacap.org

The AACAP is a great resource for addressing any number of psychiatric disorders in children associated with ADHD.

American Academy of Pediatrics (AAP)

http://www.aap.org

The AAP Web site provides information on a variety of childhood disorders.

Attention Deficit Disorder Association (ADDA)

http://www.add.org

The ADDA is a good resource for information on ADHD related subjects. It also provides resources for referral to professional support groups.

Behavior Management

http://www.disciplinehelp.com

This Web site details discipline models for handling behavior problems in the classroom and at home.

Bipolar Child Newsletter

http://www.bipolarchild.com

Bipolar Child Newsletter articles are written for parents and educators about new developments in the field of early-onset bipolar disorder and the medications used to treat the condition. The newsletter is distributed for free and has a subscription list of more than 24,000 parents and professionals.

Center for Disease Control and Prevention (CDC)— Attention-Deficit/Hyperactivity Disorder

http://www.cdc.gov/ncbddd/adhd

The CDC is one of the major operating components of the Department of Health and Human Services. Their Web site on ADHD provides updated information on this disorder.

Center on the Social and Emotional Foundations for Early Learning

http://www.vanderbilt.edu/csefel

The Center on the Social and Emotional Foundations for Early Learning is a national center focused on strengthening the capacity of child care and head start programs to improve the social and emotional outcomes of young children. Training resources are available to download in both English and Spanish.

Children and Adults With Attention/Hyperactivity Disorder (CHADD)

http://www.chadd.org

CHADD works to improve the lives of people with ADHD through education, advocacy, and support. The Web site includes factsheets, legislative information, research studies, and links.

Conduct Disorders

http://www.conductdisorders.com

The Conduct Disorders Web site has a parent message board that provides resources and information on oppositional-defiant disorder (ODD), conduct disorder (CD), and ADHD.

Council for Exceptional Children

http://www.cec.sped.org

The Council of Exceptional Children Web site is a national resource for educators and parents. The Web site has articles and news along with an extensive store full of books for teachers, parents, and students with disabilities.

Council for Exceptional Children (CEC) Division of Early Childhood

http://www.dec-sped.org

This is a division of the Council for Exceptional Children that advocates for individuals who work with and on behalf of children with special needs from birth through age eight and their families.

Easy Essay

http://www.easyessay.com

Easy Essay is an online electronic essay organizational tool that supports the basic writing process for students from upper elementary to college level. Sentence prompts and sentence frames help the student to write cohesive multiparagraph essays.

Focus Adolescent Services

http://www.focusas.com

Focus Adolescent Services is a clearinghouse for links and referrals to organizations, books, residential programs, and much more. There is a lot of information on parenting style and methods as well as behavioral problems and other adolescent issues.

Graphic Organizers for all Types of Instructional Needs

http://www.teachervision.fen.com/graphic-organizers/printable/6293.html

This Web site provides a collection of ready-to-use graphic organizers that children can use to classify ideas and communicate more effectively. The free printable graphic organizers provided at this site are designed to facilitate understanding of key concepts by allowing students to drill down to the basic points and ideas.

HealthTalk: ADHD

http://www2.healthtalk.com/go/adhd

Health Talk is a Web site for teachers and parents (includes videos, questions from parents, and articles by professionals and parents on ADHD).

Intervention Central

http://www.interventioncentral.org

Intervention Central is a Web site looking at tips and educational interventions for teachers (tools for teachers, site topics, and information workshops).

Inspiration/Kidspiration

http://www.inspiration.com

Inspiration/Kidspiration is an electronic graphic organizing program that supports students in elementary through high school with writing projects. The program offers brainstorming, clustering, outlining, and visual support for content development in the writing process.

LdPride

http://www.LdPride.net

The LdPride Web site provides information for individuals with learning disabilities including information on learning styles.

Learning Disability Association

http://www.ldonline.org

The Learning Disability Association Web site is a highly informative resource for teachers, parents, and students with learning disabilities. The site contains numerous articles and links to support individuals with learning differences.

Learning Disability Association of America (LDA)

http://www.ldanatl.org

The LDA's purpose is to advance the education and general welfare of children who show handicaps of a perceptual, conceptual, or coordinative nature.

MentalHelp.net: ADHD

http://www.mentalhelp.net/poc/center_index.php?id=3

MentalHelp.net provides users with a message board (articles, resources) on ADHD.

National Alliance on Mental Illness (NAMI)

http://www.nami.org

NAMI provides support groups and advocacy (in particular, click on the Child & Adolescent Action Center tab).

National Association of Special Education Teachers (NASET)

http://www.naset.org

The NASET Web site has numerous resources for special education teachers and professionals who work with special education students.

National Center for Learning Disabilities

http://www.ncld.org

The National Center for Learning Disabilities Web site contains sections for parents, advocates, teachers, and individuals with learning disabilities. This is an informative site with information on the latest research and on response to intervention models of early intervention.

National Institute of Mental Health (NIMH)

http://www.nimh.nih.gov

NIMH is part of the U.S. Public Health Service involved in research in juvenile emotional, cognitive, and behavioral disorders.

Positive Behavioral Interventions and Supports

http://www.pbis.org

The Technical Assistance Center for PBIS was established by the office of Special Education Program, U.S. Department of Education, to give schools capacity-building information and technical assistance for identifying, adapting, and sustaining effective schoolwide disciplinary practices. The center provides information at the level of individual students, schools, and districts that schoolwide positive behavior intervention and supports are feasible and effective.

Positive Discipline

http://positivediscipline.com

This is a Web site by Jane Nelson, EdD, on positive discipline for educators. It provides information on her workshops, articles, and videos on positive discipline.

Read Please

http://www.readplease.com

Read Please provides free text-to-speech software that allows student to highlight text on the computer screen, including text on Web site pages, and reads it out loud to the student.

Social Stories

http://www.thegraycenter.org

Social Stories from the Gray Center provide philosophy of teaching specific behaviors through social stories.

TeachingLD

http://www.teachingld.org

TeachingLD is a service of the Division for Learning Disabilities (DLD) of the Council for Exceptional Children. TeachingLD is a Web site that provides trustworthy and up-to-date resources about teaching students with learning disabilities. TeachingLD.org also publishes content about assessment, instruction, and policy related to learning disabilities.

Touch Math

http://www.touchmath.com

Touch Math is a multimodality math program that meets the needs of kinesthetic learners through a touch-point instructional process. This successful program has been used in special education programs to teach math fluency for many years.

WebMD ADD and ADHD Health Center

http://www.webmd.com/add-adhd

WebMD is an excellent Web site for a broad range of information on ADHD (medical, treatment, and Q&A sections).

Resource B

Recommended Books for Teachers

Lougy, R. A., DeRuvo, S., & Rosenthal, D. (2007). *Teaching young children with ADHD: Successful strategies and practical interventions for preK–3.* Thousand Oaks, CA: Corwin.

Parker, H. C. (1991). *ADAPT: Attention deficit accommodations plan for teaching.* Plantation, FL: Specialty Press.

Parker, H. C. (1994). *ADD hyperactivity workbook for parents, teachers, and kids* (2nd ed.). Plantation, FL: Specialty Press.

Parker, H. (1999). *Put yourself in their shoes: Understanding teenagers with ADHD.* Plantation, FL: Specialty Press.

Phelan, T. (1996). *1, 2, 3, Magic: Effective discipline for children 2–12.* Glen Ellyn, IL: Child Management.

Quinn, P. (1995*). ADD and adolescents.* New York: Magination Press.

Quinn, P., & Stern, J. (1991). *Putting on the brakes: Young peoples' guide to understanding attention deficit hyperactive disorder.* New York: Magination Press.

Rief, S. F. (1993). *How to reach and teach ADD/ADHD children.* New York: Center for Applied Research and Education.

Rief, S. F. (2003). *The ADHD book of lists.* San Francisco: Jossey-Bass.

Rief, S. F., & Heimburge, J. (1996). *How to reach and teach all students in the inclusive classroom.* Paramus, NJ: Center for Applied Research in Education.

Schetter, P. (2004). *Learning the R.O.P.E.S. for improved executive function.* Woodland, CA: Autism and Behavior Training Associates.

Taylor, J. (1994). *Helping your hyperactive/attention deficit child.* Rocklin, CA: Prima.

Resource C

Recommended Books for Parents

Barkley, R. A. (1995). *Taking charge of ADHD: The complete authoritative guide for parents.* New York: Guilford Press.

Barkley, R. A., & Robin, A. L. (2008). *Your defiant teen: 10 steps to resolve conflict and rebuild your relationship.* New York: Guilford Press.

Bradley, M. J. (2002). *Yes, your teen is crazy: Loving your kid without losing your mind.* Gig Harbor, WA: Harbor Press.

Cohen, C. (2000). *Raising your child's social IQ.* Silver Springs, MD: Advantage Press.

Comings, D. E. (2001). *Tourette syndrome and human behavior* (2nd ed.) Duarte, CA: Hope Press.

Cox, A. J. (2006). *Boys of few words: Raising our sons to communicate and connect.* New York: Guilford Press.

Dendy, C. A. (2006). *Teenagers with ADD and ADHD: A guide for parents and professionals* (2nd ed.). Bethesda, MD: Woodbine House.

Edwards, C. D. (1999). *How to handle a hard-to-handle kid: A parent's guide to understanding and changing problem behaviors.* Minneapolis, MN: Free Spirit.

Faraone, S. (2003). *Straight talk about your child's mental health: What to do when something seems wrong.* New York: Guilford Press.

Garber, S. W., Garber, M. D., & Spizman, R. F. (1996). *Beyond Ritalin: Facts about medication and other strategies for helping children, adolescents, and adults with attention deficit disorders.* New York: Harper Perennial.

Goldstein, S., Brooks, R., & Weiss, S. (2004). *Angry children, worried parents: Seven steps to help families manage anger.* North Branch, MN: Specialty Press.

Goldstein, S., & Goldstein, M. (1992). *Hyperactivity: Why won't my child pay attention?* Salt Lake City, UT: Neurology, Learning, and Behavior Center.

Greene, R. (2005). *The explosive child* (3rd ed.). New York: HarperCollins.

Hallowell, E., & Ratey, J. (1994). *Driven to distraction: Recognizing and coping with attention deficit disorder from childhood through adult.* New York: Simon & Schuster.

Hartmann, T. (1996). *ADD success stories: A guide to fulfillment for families with attention deficit disorder.* Grass Valley, CA: Underwood Books.

Hartmann, T. (1996). *Attention deficit disorder: A different perception.* Grass Valley, CA: Underwood Books.

Ingersoll, B. (1988). *Your hyperactive child*. New York: Doubleday.

Ingersoll, B., & Goldstein, M. (1993). *Attention deficit disorder and learning disabilities: Realities, myths, and controversial treatments*. New York: Doubleday.

Last, C. G. (2006). *Help your worried kids: How your child can conquer anxiety and fear*. New York: Guilford Press.

Lougy, R. A., DeRuvo, S., & Rosenthal, D. (2007). *Teaching young children with ADHD: Successful strategies and practical interventions for preK–3*. Thousand Oaks, CA: Corwin.

Lougy, R. A., & Rosenthal, D. K. (2002). *ADHD: A survival guide for parents and teachers*. Duarte, CA: Hope Press.

MacKenzie, R. (1993). *Setting limits: How to raise responsible independent children providing reasonable boundaries*. Rocklin, CA: Prima.

Miklowitz, D. J., & George, E. L. (2008). *The bipolar teen: What you can do to help your child and your family*. New York: Guilford Press.

Murphy, T., & Oberlin, L. H. (2002). *The angry child: Regaining control when your child is out of control*. New York: Three Rivers Press.

Papalos, D., & Papalos, J. (2006*). The bipolar child: The definitive and reassuring guide to childhood's most misunderstood disorder* (3rd ed.). New York: Broadway Books.

Parker, H. C. (1994). *ADD hyperactivity workbook for parents, teachers, and kids* (2nd ed.). Plantation, FL: Specialty Press.

Patterson, G. R., & Forgatch, M. (2005). *Parents and adolescents living together: Part I the basics* (2nd ed.). Champaign, IL: Research Press.

Phelan, T. (1996). *1, 2, 3, Magic: Effective discipline for children 2–12*. Glen Ellyn, IL: Child Management.

Silver, L. (1993). *Dr. Larry Silver's advice to parents on attention-deficit hyperactivity disorder*. Washington, DC: American Psychiatric Press.

Taylor, J. (1994). *Helping your hyperactive attention deficit child*. Rocklin, CA: Prima.

Wodrich, D. (1994). *What every parent wants to know: Attention deficit hyperactivity disorder*. Baltimore: Brookes.

Resource D

Recommended Books for Children

Dixon, E., & Nadeau, K. (1991). *Learning to slow down and pay attention*. Chesapeake, MD: Psychological Services.

Galvin, M. (1995). *Otto learns about his medicine: A story about medication for children* (Rev. ed.). New York: Magination Press.

Gehret, J. (1991). *Eagle's eyes: A child's view of ADD*. Fairport, NY: Verbal Images Press.

Gehret, J. (1992). *I'm somebody too*. Fairport, New York: GSI.

Gordon, M. (1992). *I would if I could*. De Witt, New York: GSI.

Gordon, M. (1992). *Jumpin' Johnny get back to work! A guide's guide to ADHD/hyperactivity*. De Witt, NY: GSI.

Gordon, M. (1992). *My brother's a world class pain*. De Witt, New York: GSI.

Levine, M. (1990). *Keeping a head in school*. Cambridge, MA: Educators.

Moss, D. (1989). *Shelly the hyperactive turtle*. Bethesda, MD: Woodbine House.

Nadeau, K. G. (1994). *Survival guide for college students with ADD or LD*. New York: Magination Press.

Parker, R. (1992). *Making the grade: An adolescent's struggle with attention deficit disorder*. Plantation, FL: Impact.

Quinn, P. (1994). *ADD and the college student*. New York: Magination Press.

Quinn, P., & Stern, J. (1991). *Putting on the brakes: Young peoples' guide to understanding attention deficit hyperactive disorder*. New York: Magination Press.

Taylor, J. (2006). *The survival guide for kids with ADD or ADHD*. Minneapolis, MN: Free Press.

Resource E

Childhood Disorders and Conditions
That Can Mimic ADHD

The disorders and conditions listed here have been found to mimic ADHD and are sometimes mistaken for ADHD.

- Adjustment disorder (move or school changes)
- Anxiety disorder
- Bipolar disorder
- Child abuse (sexual, physical, mental)
- Depression
- Fragile X syndrome
- Hyperthyroidism
- Language-based disorder
- Malnourishment or sleep deprivation (including sleep apnea)
- Mild cerebral palsy
- Mild seizure disorder
- Oppositional-defiant disorder
- Pervasive developmental disorder
- Pinworm infection
- Post-traumatic stress disorder
- Reaction to medication
- Reactive attachment disorder
- Regulatory disorder
- Sensory deficits
- Sensory integration dysfunction
- Separation anxiety disorder
- Temperament (bad fit with the environment)
- Tourette syndrome
- Unidentified learning disability

References

Alexander-Roberts, C. (1995). *A parent's guide to making it through the tough years: ADHD and teens: Proven techniques for handling emotional, academic, and behavioral problems.* Dallas, TX: Taylor.

American Psychiatric Association. (2000). *Diagnostic and statistical manual of mental disorders* (Revised 4th ed.). Washington, DC: Author.

Anastopoulos, A. D., & Shelton, T. L. (2001). *Assessing attention-deficit/hyperactivity disorder.* New York: Kluwer Academic.

Armstrong, T. (1995). *The myth of the ADHD child.* New York: Dutton Press.

Arnold L. E., Bozzolo H., Hollway J., Cook, A., DiSilvestro, R., Bozzolo, D., et al. (2005). Serum zinc correlates with parent and teacher rated inattention in children with attention-deficit/hyperactivity disorder. *Journal of Child and Adolescent Psychopharmacology, 15*(4), 628–636.

Arnsten, A. F., Steere, J. C., & Hunt, R. D. (1996). The contribution of alpha2-noradrenergic mechanisms of prefrontal cortical cognitive function: Potential significance for attention-deficit hyperactivity disorder. *Archives of General Psychiatry, 53,* 448–455.

Auiler, J. F., Liu, K., Lynch, J. M., & Gelotte, C. K. (2002). Effect of food on early drug exposure from extended-release stimulants: Results from the Concerta® (A), Adderall XRa, food evaluation (CAFA%) study. *Current Medical Research Opinion, 18,* 311–316.

Barkley, R. A. (1990). *Attention-deficit hyperactivity disorder: A handbook for diagnosis and treatment.* New York: Guilford Press.

Barkley, R. A. (1995). *Taking charge of ADHD: The complete authoritative guide for parents.* New York: Guilford Press.

Barkley, R. A. (1997). *ADHD and the nature of self-control.* New York: Guilford Press.

Barkley, R. A. (2000). *Taking charge of ADHD: The complete authoritative guide for parents* (Rev. ed.). New York: Guilford Press.

Barkley, R. A., Fischer, M., Edebrook, C. S., & Smallish, L. (1990). The adolescent outcome of hyperactive children diagnosed by research criteria: I. An 8-year prospective follow-up study. *Journal of American Academy of Child and Adolescent Psychiatry, 29,* 546–557.

Barkley, R. A., & Robin, A. L. (2008). *Your defiant teen: 10 steps to resolve conflict and rebuild your relationship.* New York: Guilford Press.

Batsche, G., Elliot, J., Graden, J. L., Grimes, J., Kovaleski, J. E., Prasse, D., et al. (2005). *Response to intervention: Policy considerations and implementation.* Washington, DC: National Association of State Directors of Special Education.

Batshaw, M. (2002). *Children with disabilities*. Baltimore: Brookes.

Biederman, J., Faraone, S. V., Keenan, K., Benjamin, J., Krifcher, B., Moore, C., et al. (1992). Further evidence for family-genetic risk factors in attention-deficit hyperactivity disorder: Patterns of comorbidity in probands and relatives of psychiatrically and pediatrically referred samples. *Archives of General Psychiatry, 49*, 728–738.

Biederman, J., Faraone, S. V., Monuteaux, M., Plunkett, E., Gifford, J., & Spencer, T. (2003). Growth deficits and ADHD revisited: Impact of gender, development, and treatment. *Pediatrics, 111*, 1010-1016.

Biederman, J., Faraone, S. V., Spencer, J. J., Mick, E. Monuteaux, M. C., & Aleardi, M. (2006). Functional impairments in adults with self-reports of diagnosed ADHD: A controlled study of 1001 adults in the community. *Journal of Clinical Psychiatry, 67*(4), 524–540.

Biederman, J., Mick, E., & Faraone, S. V. (2000). Age-dependent decline of symptoms of attention deficit hyperactivity disorder: Impact of remission definition and symptom type. *American Journal of Psychiatry, 157*(5), 816–818.

Biederman, J., Petty, C. R., Fried, R., Kaiser, R., Dolan C. R., Schoenfeld, S., et al. (2008). Educational and occupational underattainment in adults with attention-deficit/hyperactivity disorder: A controlled study. *Journal of Clinical Psychiatry, 69*(8), 1217–1222.

Biederman, J., Seidman, L. J., Petty, C. R., Fried, R., Doyle, A. E., Cohen, D. R., et al. (2008). Effects of stimulant medication on neuropsychological functioning in young adults with attention-deficit hyperactivity disorder. *Journal of Clinical Psychiatry, 69*(7), 1150–1156.

Biederman, J., Spencer, T., & Faraone, S. (2003). *Extended-release mixed amphetamine salts in ADHD: Growth parameters analysis*. Program and abstracts of the Annual Meeting of the American Psychiatric Association. San Francisco, California.

Blackman, J. A. (1999). Attention-deficit/hyperactivity disorder in preschoolers: Does it exist and should we treat it? *Pediatric Clinics of North America, 46*, 1011–1025.

Bloomquist, M. L. (1996). *Skills training for children with behavior disorders: A parent and therapist handbook*. New York: Guilford Press.

Breggin, P. R. (1998). *Talking back to Ritalin: What doctors aren't telling you about stimulants for children*. Monroe, ME: Common Courage Press.

Brown, T. E. (2008, February). Executive functions: Describing six aspects of a complex syndrome. *Attention, 15*(1), 12–17.

Bukstein, O. G. (2006). Current opinions and new developments in the pharmacology treatment of ADHD. *Remedica, 1*(1), 8–15.

Burgess, J. R. (1998, September 2–3). *Attention deficit hyperactivity disorder: Observational and interventional studies*. Paper presented at the National Institutes of Health Workshop on Omega-3 Essential Fatty Acids and Psychiatric Disorders, Bethesda, MD.

Chappell, P. B., Phillip, B., Riddle, M. A., Scahill, L., Lynch, A., Schults, R., et al. (1995, September). Guanfacine treatment of comorbid attention-deficit hyperactivity disorder and Tourette's syndrome: Preliminary clinical experience. *Journal of American Academy of Child and Adolescent Psychiatry, 34*, 1140–1146.

Colquhoun, I., & Bunday, S. (1981). A lack of essential fatty acids as a possible cause of hyperactivity in children. *Medical Hypothesis, 7*, 673–679.

Comings, D. E. (2001). *Tourette syndrome and human behavior* (2nd ed.). Duarte, CA: Hope Press.

Comings, D. E. (2008). *Did man create God? Is your spiritual brain at peace with your thinking brain?* Duarte, CA: Hope Press.

Conners, C. K., Casat, C. D., Gualtieri, C. T., & Weller, E. M. (1996). Bupropion hydrochloride in attention deficit disorder with hyperactivity. *Journal of the American Academy of Child and Adolescent Psychiatry, 35,* 1314–1321.

Conroy, M., Sutherland, K., Snyder, A., & Marsh, S. (2008). Classwide interventions: Effective instruction makes a difference. *Teaching Exceptional Children, 40*(6), 24–30.

Current ADHD insights: A summary of recent presentations on ADHD. (2004, February). Hasbrouck Heights, NJ: MedLearning.

Denckla, M. B. (2007). Executive function: Binding together the definitions of attention-deficit/hyperactivity disorder and learning disabilities. In L. Meltzer (Ed.), *Executive function in education: From theory to practice.* New York: Guilford Press.

Denham, S. A. (1998). *Emotional development in young children.* New York: Guilford Press.

Diener, M. B., & Milich, R. (1997). Effects of positive feedback on the social interactions of boys with attention deficit hyperactivity disorder: A test of self-protective hypothesis. *Journal of Clinical Child Psychology, 26*(3), 256–265.

Doyle, A. E. (2006). Executive functions in attention-deficit/hyperactivity disorder. *Journal of Clinical Psychiatry, 67*(8), 21–26.

Dreikers, R. (1964). *Children: The challenge.* New York: Hawthorn Books.

Dunn, R., & Dunn, K. (1978). *Teaching students through their individual learning styles: A practical approach.* Reston, VA: Reston.

Egger, J., Stella, A., & McEwen, L. (1992). Controlled trial of hyposensitification with food-induced hyperkinetic syndrome. *Lancet, 334,* 1150–1153.

Endo, T., Sugiyama, T., & Someya, T. (2006). Attention-deficit/hyperactivity disorder and dissociative disorder among abused children. *Psychiatry and Clinical Neuroscience, 60*(4), 434–438.

Erhardt, D., & Hinshaw, S. P. (1994). Initial sociometric impressions of attention-deficit hyperactivity disorder and comparison boys: Predictions from social behaviors and from nonbehavioral variables. *Journal of Consulting and Clinical Psychology, 62*(4), 833–842.

Fairbanks, S., Simonsen, B., & Sugai, G, (2008). Classwide secondary and tertiary tier practices and systems. *Teaching Exceptional Children, 40*(6), 44–52.

Faraone, S. V., Biederman, J., Spencer, T., Mick, E., Murray, K., Petty, C., et al. (2006). Diagnosing adult attention deficit hyperactivity disorder: Are late onset and subthreshold diagnoses valid? *American Journal of Psychiatry, 163*(10), 1720–1729.

Findling, R. L., Arnold, E., Greenhill, L. L., Kratochvil, C. J., & McGough, J. J. (2007). Commentary: Diagnosing and managing complicated ADHD. *Journal of Clinical Psychiatry, 68,* 1963–1969.

Fink-Chorzempka, B., Graham, S., Harris, K. R. 2005. What can I do to help young children who struggle with writing? *Teaching Exceptional Children, 37*(5), 64–66.

Firestone, P., Musten, L. M., Pisterman, S., Mercer, J., & Bennett, S. (1998). Short-term side effects of stimulant medication are increased in preschool children with attention-deficit hyperactivity disorder: A double-blind placebo-controlled study. *Journal of Child and Adolescent Psychopharmacology, 8,* 13–25.

Friend, M., & Cook, L. (2003). *Interactions: Collaboration skills for school professionals* (4th ed.). Boston: Allyn & Bacon.

Garber, S. W., Garber, M. D., & Spizman, R. F. (1996). *Beyond Ritalin: Facts about medication and other strategies for helping children, adolescents, and adults with attention deficit disorders.* New York. Harper Perennial.

Gardner, H. (1993). *Frames of mind: The theory of multiple intelligences* (10th ed.). New York: Basic Books.

Goldman, L. S., Genel, M., Bezman, R. J., & Slanetz, P. J. (1998). Diagnosis and treatment of attention-deficit/hyperactivity disorder in children and adolescents. *Journal of the American Medical Association, 279*(14), 1100–1107.

Goldstein, S., & Goldstein, M. (1990). *Managing attention disorders in children: A guide for practitioners.* New York: John Wiley & Sons.

Good T., & Grouws, D. (1977). Teaching effects: A process-product study in fourth grade mathematics classrooms. *Journal of Teacher Education, 28*(3), 49–54.

Gray Center of Social Learning and Understanding. (2006).*What are social stories?* Retrieved on November 1, 2006, from http://www.thegraycenter.org/store/index.cfm?fuseaction=page.display&page_id=30.

Greenhill, L., Kollins, S., Abikoff, H., McCracken, J., Riddle, M., Swanson, J. (2006). Efficacy and safety of immediate-release methylphenidate treatment for preschoolers with ADHD. *Journal of the American Academy of Child and Adolescent Psychiatry, 45*(11), 1284–1293.

Gregory, G. H., & Chapman, C. (2007). *Differentiated instruction strategies: One size doesn't fit all* (2nd ed.). Thousand Oaks, CA: Corwin.

Hawken, L., & Horner, R. (2003). Evaluation of a targeted group intervention within a schoolwide system of behavior support. *Journal of Behavioral Education, 12,* 225–240.

Hechtman, L. (1996). Families of children with attention deficit hyperactivity disorder: A review. *Canadian Journal of Psychiatry, 41*(6), 350–360.

Hoagwood, K., Jensen, P. S., Feil, M., Benedetto, V., & Bhatara, V. S. (2000, October). Medication management of stimulants in pediatric practice settings: A national perspective. *Journal of Developmental and Behavioral Pediatrics, 21*(5), 322–331.

Hooper, S. R., & Umansky, W. (2004). *Young children with special needs.* Upper Saddle River, NJ: Pearson Education.

Horner, R. H. (2007). *Discipline prevention data.* Eugene, OR: OSEP Center on Positive Behavioral Interventions and Supports, University of Oregon.

Horrobin, D. F., Glen, A. I., & Hudson, C. J. (1995). Possible relevance of phospholipid abnormalities and genetic interactions in psychiatric disorders: The relationship between dyslexia and schizophrenia. *Med Hypotheses, 45*(6), 605–613.

Hughes, J., & DeForest, P. (1993). Consultant directiveness and support as predictors of consultation outcomes. *Journal of School Psychology, 31*(3), 355–373.

Hughes, J., Grossman, P., & Barker, D. (1990). Teacher expectancies, participation in consultation, and perceptions of consultant helpfulness. *School Psychology Quarterly, 5,* 167–179.

Hunt, R. D., Armsten, A. F., & Asbell, M. D. (1995). An open trial of Guanfacine in the treatment of attention-deficit hyperactivity disorder. *Journal of the American Academy of Child and Adolescent Psychiatry, 34*(1), 50–54.

Individuals With Disabilities Education Improvement Act of 2004, 20 U.S.C § 1400 (2004).

Kampwirth, T. J. (2006). *Collaborative consultation in the schools: Effective practices for students with learning and behavior problems.* New Jersey: Pearson.

Kelleher, K. J., McInerny, T. K., Gardner, W. P., Childs, G., & Wasserman, R. C. (2000, June). Increasing identification of psychosocial problems: 1979–1996. *Pediatrics, 105*(6), 1313–1321.

Konofal, E., Cortese, S., Lecendreux, M., Arnulf, I., & Mouren, M. C. (2005). Effectiveness of iron supplementation in a young child with attention-deficit/hyperactivity disorder. *Pediatrics, 116*(5), e732–e734.

Kozielec, T., & Starobrat-Hermelin B. (1997). Assessment of magnesium levels in children with attention deficit hyperactivity disorder (ADHD). *Magnesium Research, 10*(2), 143–148.

Lavoie, R. (1996). *Learning disabilities and discipline with Richard Lavoie: When chips are down . . . strategies for improving children's behavior: A program guide.* Washington, DC: Learning Disabilities Project at WETA.

Lavoie, R. (2005). *It's so much work to be your friend: Helping the child with learning disabilities find social success.* New York: Touchstone Press.

Layey, B. B., Pelham, W. E., Stein, M. A., Loney, J., Trapani, C., Nugent, K., et al. (1998). Validity of DSM-IV attention-deficit/hyperactivity disorder for younger children. *Journal of the American Academy of Child and Adolescent Psychiatry, 37*(7), 695–702.

ldonline.org. (n.d.). ADHD basics: *Other disorders that sometimes accompany ADHD.* Retrieved October 21, 2008, from http://www.ldonline.org/adhdbasics/other.

Levine, M. (1993). *Developmental variation and learning disorders.* Cambridge, MA: Educator's.

Levine, M. (2002). *A mind at a time.* New York: Simon & Schuster.

Lougy, R., DeRuvo, S., & Rosenthal, D. (2007). *Teaching young children with ADHD: Successful strategies and practical interventions for preK–3.* Thousand Oaks, CA: Corwin.

Lougy, R., & Rosenthal, D. K. (2002). *ADHD: A survival guide for parents and teachers.* Duarte, CA: Hope Press.

Lyon, M. R., Cline, J. C., Totosy de Zepetnek, J., Shan, J. J., Pang, P., & Benishin, C. (2001). Effect of the herbal extract combination Panax quinquefolium and gingko biloba on attention deficit hyperactivity disorder: A pilot study. *Journal of Psychiatry Neuroscience, 26*(3), 221–228.

Mariani, M., & Barkley, R. A. (1997). Neuropsychological and academic functioning in preschool children with attention-deficit hyperactivity disorder. *Developmental Neuropsychology, 13,* 111–129.

Mayes, S. D., & Calhoun, S. L. (2006). Frequency of reading, math and writing disabilities in children with clinical disorders. *Learning and Individual Differences, 16*(2), 145–157.

McCann, D., Barrett, A., Cooper, A., Crumpler, D., Dalen, L., Grimshaw, K., et al. (2007). Food additives and hyperactive behavior in 3-year-old and 8/9-year-old children in the community: A randomized, double-blinded, placebo-controlled trial. *Lancet, 370*(9598), 1560–1567.

Meltzer, L. (Ed.). (2007). *Executive function in education: From theory to practice.* New York: Guilford Press.

Meltzer, L., & Krishnan, K., (2007). Executive function difficulties and learning disabilities: Understandings and misunderstandings. In L. Meltzer (Ed.), *Executive function in education: From theory to practice.* New York: Guilford Press.

Michigan ranks third in nation in prescribing Ritalin: Some say schools turn to medication to control students. Ritalin's routine use raises alarm over diagnosis, goals. Use of Ritalin in schools nearly out of control. (1998, March 8). *Detroit News.*

Millstein, R. B., Wilens, T. E., Biederman, J., & Spencer, T. J. (1997). Presenting ADHD symptoms and subtypes in clinically referred adults with ADHD. *Journal of Attention Disorders, 2*(3), 159–166.

Minde, K. (1998). The use of psychotropic medication in preschoolers: Some recent developments. *Canadian Journal of Psychiatry, 43*, 571–575.

Mitchell, E. A., Aman, M. G., Turbott, S. H., & Manku, M. (1987). Clinical characteristics and serum essential fatty acid levels in hyperactive children. *Clinical Pediatrics, 26*(8), 406–411.

Modi, N. B., Wang, B., Hu, W. T., & Gupta, S. K. (2000). Effect of food on the pharmacokinetics of osmotic controlled-release methylphenidate HCl in healthy subjects. *Biopharmaceuticals and Drug Disposition, 21*(1), 23–31.

Morrison, G. M., Walker, D., Wakefield, P., & Solberg, S. (1994). Teacher preferences for collaborative relationships: Relationship to efficacy for teaching in prevention-related domains. *Psychology in the Schools, 31*, 221–231.

Mousain-Bosc, M., Roche, M., Polge, A., Pradal-Prat, D., Rapin, J., & Bali, J. P. (2006). Improvement of neurobehavioral disorders in children supplemented with magnesium-B6. I. Attention deficit hyperactivity disorders. *Magnesium Research, 19*(1), 46–52.

Mulrine, C. F., Prater, M. A., & Jenkins, A, (2008). The active classroom: Supporting students with attention deficit hyperactivity disorder through exercise. *Teaching Exceptional Children, 40*(5), 16–22.

Nadeau, K. G., Littman, E. B., & Quinn, P. O. (1999). *Understanding girls with ADHD.* Silver Springs, MD: Advantage Books.

Nakamura, R. (2002, September 26). *Testimony before the Committee of Government Reform.* U.S. House of Representatives OLPA Hearings, 107th Congress.

Pastor, P. N., & Reuben, C. A. (2002). Attention deficit disorder and learning disabilities: United States. *Vital and Health Statistics 10*(206), 1–12.

Pelham, W. E., McBurnett, K., Harper, G. W., Milich, R., Murphy, D. A., Clinton, J., et al. (1990). Methylphenidate and baseball playing in ADHD children: Who's on first? *Journal of Consulting and Clinical Psychology, 58*(1), 130–133.

Phelan, T. W. (1996). *All about attention deficit disorder: Symptoms, diagnosis and treatment: Children and adults.* Glen Ellyn, Illinois: Child Management.

Platt, A. (2006). *ADHD and math disabilities: Cognitive similarities and instructional interventions.* Retrieved on July 17, 2008, from http://research.aboutkidshealth.ca/teachadhd/resources/ADHD_and_Math_Disabilities.pdf.

Rappley, M. D., Mullan, P. B., Alvarez, F. J., Eneli, I. U., Wang, J., & Gardiner, J. C. (1999). Diagnosis of attention-deficit/hyperactivity disorder and use of psychotropic medication in very young children. *Archives of Pediatrics and Adolescent Medicine, 153*, 1039–1045.

Rehabilitation Act, Section 504, 34, C.F.R. § 104.33 (1973).

Reid, J. R., Reimberr, F. W., Marchant, B. K., Faraone, S. V., Adler, L. A., & West, S. A. (2008, February). Gender differences in 2 clinical trials of adults with attention-deficit/hyperactivity disorders: A retrospective data analysis. *Journal of Clinical Psychiatry, 69*(2), 213–221.

Richardson, A. J., & Ross, M. A. (2000). Fatty acid metabolism in neurodevelopmental disorder: A new perspective on associations between attention-deficit/hyperactivity disorder, dyslexia, dyspraxia, and the autistic spectrum. *Prostaglandins Leukot Essent Fatty Acids, 63*(1–2), 1–9.

Robin, A. L. (1998). *ADHD in adolescents: Diagnosis and treatment.* New York: Guilford Press.

Rucklidge, J. J., Brown, D. L., Crawford, S., & Kaplan, B. J. (2006). Retrospective reports of childhood trauma in adults with ADHD. *Journal of Attention Disorders, 9*(4), 631–641.

Rutherford, P. (2002). *Why didn't I learn this in college?* Alexandria, VA: Just ASK.

Sadiq, A. J. (2007, September). Attention-deficit/hyperactivity disorder and integrative approaches. *Psychiatric Annuals, 37*(9), 630–638.

Scahill, L., Chappell, P. B., Young, S. K., Schultz, R. T., Katosovich, L., Shepherd, E., et al. (2001, July). A placebo-controlled study of Guanfacine in the treatment of children with tic disorders and attention deficit hyperactivity disorder. *American Journal of Psychiatry, 158*(7), 1067–1074.

Scahill, L., & Schwab-Stone, M. (2000). Epidemiology of ADHD in school-age children. *Child and Adolescent Psychiatry Clinics of North America, 9*, 541–555.

Schetter, P. (2004). *Learning the R.O.P.E.S. for improved executive function.* Woodland, CA: Autism and Behavior Training Associates.

Shaw, P. (2007). *Brain matures a few years late in ADHD, but follows normal pattern.* National Association of Special Education Teachers. Retrieved on November 13, 2007, from http://www.naset.org/807.0.html?&tx_ttnews[backPid]=533&tx_ttnews[tt_news]=2410&cHash=d3b1768475.

Shekim, W. O., Javid, J., Dans, J. M., & Bylund, D. B. (1983). Effects of D- amphetamine on urinary metabolites on dopamine and norepinephrine in hyperactive children. *Biological Psychiatry, 18*, 707–714.

Short, E. J., Manos, M. J., Findling, R. L., & Schubel, E. A. (2004). A prospective study of stimulant response in preschool children: Insights from ROC analyses. *Journal of the American Academy of Child and Adolescent Psychiatry, 43*(3), 251–259.

Silver, L. (1992). *Attention deficit hyperactivity disorder: A clinical guide to diagnosis and treatment.* Washington, DC: American Psychiatric Press.

Smutney, J. F., & von Fremd, S. E. (2004). *Differentiating for the young child: Teaching strategies across the content areas (K–3).* Thousand Oaks, CA: Corwin.

Spencer, T., Biederman, J., Harding, M., O'Donnell, D., Faraone, S., & Wilens, T. (1996). Growth deficits in ADHD children revisited: Evidence for disorder-associated growth delays? *Journal of American Academy of Child and Adolescent Psychiatry, 35*, 1460–1469.

Spencer, T. (2003). *Group CS: Long-term once-daily OROS® methylphenidate treatment for ADHD: Evaluating effect on growth.* Program and abstracts of the Annual Meeting of the American Psychiatric Association. San Francisco, California.

Stein, M. A., Efron, L. A., Schiff, W. B., & Glanzman, M. (2002). Attention deficit and hyperactivity disorders. In M. L. Batshaw, *Children with disabilities* (5th ed.). Baltimore: Paul Brookes

Stevens, L. J., Zentall, S. S., Deck, J. L., Abate, M. L., Watkins, B. A., Lipp, S. R., et al. (1995). Essential fatty acid metabolism in boys with attention-deficit hyperactivity disorder. *American Journal of Clinical Nutrition, 62*(4), 761–768.

Sugai, G., Horner, R. H., Dunlap, G., Hieneman, M., Lewis, T. J., Nelson, C. M., et al. (2000). Applying positive behavior support and functional behavioral assessment in schools. *Journal of Positive Behavior Interventions, 2*(3), 131–143.

Sutherland, K., Alder, N., & Gunter, P. (2003). The effect of varying rates of OTR on the classroom behavior of students with EBD. *Journal of Emotional and Behavioral Disorders, 11*(4), 239–248.

Swanson, H. L., & Beebe-Frankenberger, M. (2004). The relationship between working memory and mathematical problem solving in children at risk and not at risk for serious math difficulties. *Journal of Educational Psychology, 96*(3), 471–491.

Taylor, J. (1994). *Helping your hyperactive attention deficit child.* Rocklin, CA: Prima.

Taylor, J. (2001). *From defiance to cooperation: Real solutions for transforming the angry, defiant, discouraged child.* New York: Three Rivers.

Taylor, J. (2006). *The survival guide for kids with ADD or ADHD.* Minneapolis, MN: Free Press.

Teeter, P. A. (1998). *Interventions for ADHD: Treatment in developmental context.* New York: Guilford Press.

Thurber, J. R., Heller T. L., & Hinshaw, S. P. (2002). The social behaviors and peer expectations of girls with attention deficit hyperactivity disorder and comparison girls. *Journal of Clinical Child and Adolescent Psychology, 31*(4), 443–452.

Tilly, W. D. (2008). The evolution of school psychology to science based practice. In A. Thomas & J. Grimes (Eds.), *Best practices in school psychology V.* Bethesda, MD: National Association of School Psychologists.

Tomlinson, C. A. (2000, August). *Differentiation of instruction in the elementary grades.* Retrieved on July 25, 2006, from ERIC Clearinghouse on Elementary and Early Childhood Education at http://ceep.crc.uiuc.edu/eecearchive/digests/2000/tomlin00.pdf.

Tomlinson, C. A. (2001). *How to differentiate instruction in mixed ability classrooms.* Alexandria, VA: Association for Supervision and Curriculum Development.

Toren, P., Eldar, S., Sela, B. A., Wolmer, L., Weitz, R., Inbar, D., et al. (1996). Zinc deficiency in attention-deficit hyperactivity disorder. *Biological Psychiatry, 40*(12), 1308–1310.

Vaughan, B. S., & Kratochvil, C. J. (2006). Pharmacotherapy of ADHD in young children. *Psychiatry, 3*(8), 36–45.

Vygotsky, L. (1978). *Mind and society: The development of higher mental processes.* Cambridge, MA: Harvard University Press.

Weiss, G., Hechtman, L., Milroy, T., & Periman, T. (1985). Psychiatric status of hyperactive adults: A controlled prospective 15-year follow-up in 63 hyperactive children. *Journal of the American Academy of Child Psychiatry, 24*(2), 211–220.

Wolf, L. E., & Wasserstein, J. (2001). Adult ADHD: Concluding thoughts. *Annals of the New York Academy of Science, 931*, 396–408.

Wolraich, M., Wilson, D. B., & White, J. W. (1995). The effect of sugar on behavior or cognition in children: A meta-analysis. *Journal of the American Medical Association, 274*, 1617–1621.

Zito, J. M., Safer, D. J., DosReis, S., Gardner, J. F., Boles, C., & Frances, L. (2000). Trends in the prescribing of psychotropic medications in preschoolers. *Journal of the American Medical Association, 283*(3), 1025–1030.

Index

CORWIN
A SAGE Company

The Corwin logo—a raven striding across an open book—represents the union of courage and learning. Corwin is committed to improving education for all learners by publishing books and other professional development resources for those serving the field of PreK–12 education. By providing practical, hands-on materials, Corwin continues to carry out the promise of its motto: **"Helping Educators Do Their Work Better."**